EMBRACING POSSIBILITIES

Nurturing Children With Special Needs

I0152987

Vanesia Bowden

ISBN: 978-1-958443-51-4 (paperback)

Scripture quotations marked "KJV" are taken from the Holy Bible, King James Version (Public Domain).

Scripture quotations marked (NIV) are taken from the Holy Bible, New International Version®, NIV®. Copyright © 1973, 1978, 1984 by Biblica, Inc.™ Used by permission of Zondervan. All rights reserved worldwide.

FOREWORD

In the world of parenting, there exists a complex journey that transcends the ordinary, one marked by resilience, compassion, empathy, and an unwavering commitment to embracing possibilities.

The burden of stress is great for parents of those with special needs, but within those challenges lies a profound invitation for all of us to redefine our understanding of ability, resilience, and the very foundation of what it means to be a family.

"Embracing Possibilities: Nurturing Children with Special Needs" is a comprehensive and compassionate resource for parents and caregivers who are committed to providing the best possible care and support for children with special needs.

It is a powerful and timely guide, a roadmap useful for navigating uncharted territories, offering insights, guidance, and a sense of solidarity for those who may sometimes feel isolated in their experiences.

The book covers a wide range of topics: diagnosis and intervention, education and inclusion, family and community involvement, anchoring hope, and nurturing faith. It, therefore, is a beacon of wisdom, knowledge, empowerment, and encouragement for all those traversing this unique landscape.

The author of this book has done an excellent job of providing practical advice and guidance for parents and caregivers. As I reflect upon its pages, I am reminded of the power inherent in the human spirit and the boundless love that propels parents, caregivers, and educators forward on this transformative path. Each page illuminates the strength that arises from facing adversity head-on and the transformative power of love and community.

"Embracing Possibilities" is more than a book; it is a community, a source of strength, and a reservoir of hope. Its call to reflection and affirmation ensures learning and interaction are taking place.

I commend the author, *Vanesia Bowden*, for her dedication and commitment to this important body of work. She has created a resource that will be of great value to all the stakeholders of children with special needs and will constantly remind parents that they are not alone on this journey.

It is my honor to introduce you to this body of work. May it serve as a guiding light for all those who believe in the transformative power of love and the infinite possibilities that lie within each and every child.

I sincerely hope readers will find solace, inspiration, and practical guidance in this book. I am honored to be a part of this project, and I hope this book will be a source of inspiration and empowerment for many years to come. It is a must-read.

Chevonette James-Henry
Special Education Teacher (B.S.Ed.)
Author, Mentor, Motivational Speaker

PREFACE

It is a heartwarming journey for me to bring this book, *Embracing Possibilities: Nurturing Children with Special Needs*, into your hands. This endeavor has been a long-cherished dream that took root deep within my heart many years ago, back in 2015. It is a dream that has always been entwined with my passion for speaking up for those who often find themselves marginalized, overlooked, and without a voice.

You see, I have been a quiet advocate from a young age. I would stand up for those who couldn't speak for themselves, even if it meant getting into a bit of trouble. Strangely, I couldn't understand why I felt so strongly about it. Little did I know that this was all part of a greater purpose, slowly being unveiled in my life. Would you believe I would not even ask a question in class?

Writing this book has been a surprise in many ways. Back in 2018, when my child received his diagnosis, I found myself in a place of profound silence. It was an unspoken pain that I carried as a parent and a passionate advocate. I was committed to doing all the right things during my pregnancy. I am an intentional parent with a background in healthcare. I prayed, fasted, and sowed seeds of faith throughout those nine months, believing I was ensuring my child's bright future. Yet, the diagnosis shattered my expectations and left me with countless questions for the God I serve.

As time passed, the daily challenges and routines swept me away, and I almost forgot my deep desire to write. I busied myself with my blog for three years, not realizing that the true calling had merely been resting, waiting for the right moment to emerge.

Towards the end of 2022, my heavenly Father, whom I lovingly call "Abba," gently reminded me of my calling to write. I embarked on a journey to figure out how to proceed, as my perfectionist tendencies wanted a fully detailed plan. But Abba, in His wisdom, firmly nudged me to start writing immediately. That was when this book began to take shape. It wasn't the book I had initially started, but it was the book God wanted for such a time as this. I prayed and fasted, seeking divine guidance for the structure and content. The result is the book you hold today, one that I said yes to timidly and with many prayers.

I pray that **Embracing Possibilities** touches your heart and life, as it is designed to be a blessing, a guiding light, and a source of encouragement. May you find the strength and resilience to nurture your children with special needs and encounter the same divine presence that has led me on this incredible journey.

As you delve into these pages, may you also encounter my Abba and His Holy Spirit, who offers comfort, wisdom, and boundless love.

Many blessings to you and your family, dear reader.

With warmth and gratitude,

Vanesia

HOW TO USE THIS BOOK

This book was created with you, the loving and dedicated parent of a special needs child, in mind. I understand the demands on your time and energy and have designed this book to be a practical and easy-to-read resource.

The three main features are:

1. **Straight to the Point**. We know your time is valuable. That is why I went straight to the heart of the matter, providing content that is both concise and relevant. My goal is to provide you with the information you need without unnecessary fluff.

2. **Interactive Learning**. As a seasoned teacher and trainer with specialized training in special education, I believe that true education should improve the quality of life. That is why you will find several interactive elements throughout this book:

   a) **Reflection Prompts:** After reading a section, take a moment to reflect on how the information applies to your unique situation. Consider the practical implications of what you have learned.
   b) **Affirmations:** The power of positive words is immense. Affirmations can shape your mindset and actions. Use them as a source of encouragement and strength.

c) **Thoughts to Ponder:** You will discover thought-provoking scriptures and famous quotes that are meant to inspire and uplift you. Take a moment to contemplate these meaningful words.

d) **Note to Self:** If something stands out to you or if there is a particular area you are eager to explore further, jot down your thoughts here. This section is for your personal reflections and questions.

e) **Self-Care Corner:** Express your insights and takeaways creatively in this corner. Whether it is a heartfelt prayer, a poem, or any other form of creative expression, let it be a reminder of the role your creativity can play on your journey.

3. **Empowerment and Growth.** I sincerely hope and pray that this book will empower you and contribute to your personal growth as you continue to nurture your special needs child. You are not alone on this journey; together, we can embrace the endless possibilities.

ACKNOWLEDGMENTS

I want to express my deepest gratitude to the Almighty, my Abba, for inspiring and sustaining me throughout this project. Your guidance, strength, and unwavering love have been my constant source of inspiration.

I extend my heartfelt appreciation to my family and friends for your unwavering support and encouragement. Your belief in me and this project has been a driving force in bringing it to fruition.

A special thanks to those who prayed with me during the entire process. Your prayers have been a powerful source of motivation and strength.

I am deeply thankful for the countless individuals and experts in the field of special education who have shared their knowledge and experiences, shaping the content of this book.

Last but not least, I want to acknowledge and express my immense appreciation to the parents and caregivers of children with special needs. Your resilience, love, and dedication are a constant source of inspiration.

DEDICATION

This book is, first and foremost, dedicated to my precious children, whose presence in my life has transformed me into the diligent and attentive mother I am today. You are my greatest teachers, and I am forever grateful for the lessons you have imparted.

I also dedicate this book to all the amazing neurodivergent/special needs young ones and their devoted loved ones. Your uniqueness, resilience, and the boundless creativity you encompass inspire me daily. May the world see you for the incredible individuals you are, and may your innovations and creativity shine brightly.

This book would not exist without you, and I am profoundly thankful for that.

A SPECIAL NOTE TO PARENTS

Warm greetings, fellow parent, on this extraordinary journey with your special needs children. It is a path that demands courage, resilience, and determination. Parenting, shaped by our unique challenges, has transformed me profoundly, and I sense a shared experience in you.

Reflecting on our journey, I have come to realize the importance of understanding our "why" in parenting. Beyond the circumstances of conception, it is about intentionally navigating the intricacies of raising a child with special needs. While some may opt for a more spontaneous approach, our circumstances require a thoughtful and deliberate strategy.

Consider this: *Why do you parent the way you do?* Ask yourself three times, going deeper with each reflection. Recognize that generic parenting strategies might not resonate with our unique situations. It is crucial to acknowledge this distinction.

Now, examine the outcomes of your parenting approach. Has it yielded the desired results? If not, embrace the opportunity to adjust and adapt. Seek motivation and information from sources attuned to our specific needs.

By answering these questions, we position ourselves to nurture our children intentionally and gracefully. This mindset becomes our anchor during challenging moments — the tantrums, the unjust judgments—empowering us to navigate our parenting journey with resilience and love.

HANNAH MOMENTS NEURODIVERSITY AND EMPOWERMENT HUB

Here, we are committed to empowering wellness and learning using our multidisciplinary expertise, unyielding passion, and creative insights.

Our Vision: Hannah Moments Neurodiversity and Empowerment Hub envisions a world where individuals experiencing neurodiversity or special needs and their caregivers find a nurturing sanctuary.

We strive to be the premier destination, offering practical, actionable information and fostering a culture of continuous learning and development. Through our expertise, passion, and creativity, we aim to empower every individual to lead a fulfilling and inclusive life, promoting mental, emotional, and physical wellness.

Our Mission: Our mission is to provide a comprehensive and compassionate platform. We endeavor to deliver valuable insights, practical guidance, and tailored resources that enhance the everyday lives of individuals experiencing neurodiversity and special needs.

We are dedicated to promoting lifelong learning, nurturing personal growth, and instilling a sense of purpose and belonging, all of which contribute to holistic wellness. Leveraging our multi-disciplinary expertise and unwavering passion, we strive to be a beacon of support, understanding, and empowerment for overall well-being.

Our Goals:

- Empowerment through Education
- Building a Supportive Community
- Enhanced Accessibility and Inclusivity
- Collaborative Partnerships
- Newsletter and Outreach

Our Services include a website with valuable information written in simple terms that all can benefit from. Additionally, we offer:

- Coaching for parents of special needs children.
- Coaching for special needs children.
- Teacher training for inclusive education.
- Organization training for inclusivity.
- Speaker and trainer on neurodiversity and inclusion.

TABLE OF CONTENTS

INTRODUCTION

EMBRACING THE JOURNEY

Each person on earth embarks on a unique journey, a voyage through time and experience that shapes who they are and what they become. Our paths are as diverse as the stars in the night sky, each one bearing its own constellation of challenges and triumphs. As parents and caregivers of children diagnosed with special needs, our journey takes us through uncharted territories, where the landscapes are both breathtaking and formidable. In this profound voyage, being present in each moment becomes more than a mere sentiment—it becomes an essential practice guiding us to make the most of every day, every minute.

Life can surprise us, unfolding its mysteries in ways we could never have anticipated. We all start with expectations, dreams, and visions of what lies ahead. Yet, when the unexpected graces our path, and a diagnosis of special needs is bestowed upon our child, those preconceived notions are gently swept away, leaving us standing on the shore of a new reality. It is here, in this moment of profound shift, that the journey truly begins.

Grief may envelop us, and that is alright. Grief is a tribute to the loss of what we thought our child's life would be like—the dreams we held dear, the imagined milestones, the unwritten chapters. It is important to note that every parent, not just those of us with children diagnosed with special needs, must let go of our preconceived notions and embrace who God created our children to be. Many times, we feel as though we are alone in this area of grief, and we are not. However, what may be different is the magnitude of said emotion. Consequently, we navigate through a spectrum of emotions, from disbelief to sorrow, anger to acceptance. The tears we shed are not signs of weakness but testaments to the depth of our love and the complexities of our roles. As the waves of grief recede, they reveal a shoreline glistening with newfound strength—a strength born from embracing the truth of our circumstances and choosing to see the light even in the midst of shadows.

Embracing our children's journey does not diminish their challenges; instead, it allows us to transcend those challenges by reshaping the narrative. Our child's path is unique, and we can pave the way with acceptance and love. Just as every tree has its roots in the earth and its branches reaching for the sky, our children are deeply rooted in their individuality, and it is our privilege to nurture their growth.

To embrace the journey is to be present, to fully inhabit each moment as it unfolds. It is to hold our child's hand and walk with them, step by step, through each triumph and trial. The strength we find in ourselves, the resilience we cultivate, becomes the cornerstone of our child's foundation. We learn that every milestone, regardless of its scale, is a victory; every effort, no matter how small, is a triumph.

In these pages, we embark on a shared expedition of courage, understanding, and growth. This book is a compass, guiding us through the terrains of mindset and skillset, of challenges and celebrations. It is a tribute to the power of our love and an acknowledgment of the remarkable potential within every child. Together, we will explore the art of embracing what is, finding beauty in every moment, and nurturing the seeds of possibilities.

As we journey forward, let us keep our hearts open, our minds receptive, and our spirits unwavering. Let us remember that our children are not defined by their diagnoses; they are defined by the love we invest, the opportunities we create, and the joy we share. By embracing the journey, we become beacons of hope and beget a kinder, more inclusive, and endlessly compassionate world.

In the chapters that follow, we will delve into the depths of mindset, the intricacies of skillset, and the boundless potential that resides within our children. Together, let us embark on this odyssey, embracing the journey with unwavering love, boundless hope, and a steadfast commitment to nurturing the extraordinary in every child.

CHAPTER 1

GRIEVING AND EMBRACING THE SPECTRUM OF EMOTIONS

In all its intricacies, life often challenges us to confront emotions, feelings, and realities we never knew or expected to face. Such was my experience years ago when my son was diagnosed with special needs. Being a woman who feels deeply, I found myself caught in a whirlwind of emotions. I found myself in tears countless days, and those tears rocked me to bed. I felt a deep sense of grief and struggled to reconcile my reality. I traced my steps back to pre-pregnancy and pregnancy to see where I went wrong. What was my wrong move? Where did I go wrong? But as we grow, we learn that laying blame isn't the answer and that we will never understand the why of each situation. We face the fact that we may do everything we know is right and still experience bad and painful situations. Our minds will wonder if there is any point in doing our best. My response is an resounding yes!

Doing our best does a grand thing for us; it frees our conscience. In doing so, though, our minds wander occasionally, but we know indefinitely that we have covered our bases and our children are not suffering because of our actions. Ultimately, we are freed from guilt. Let us also recall the story of the man blind from birth; his condition was so God could be glorified.

"As he went along, he saw a man blind from birth. His disciples asked him, "Rabbi, who sinned, this man or his parents, that he was born blind? Neither this man nor his parents sinned," said Jesus, "but this happened so that the works of God might be displayed in him." (John 9:1-3 – NIV).

This showed, too, that not every unfavorable situation we experience is a result of something we did wrong. Sometimes, it is for the glory of God to be revealed. May we also sober our minds that many of these illnesses are passed through the generations through the bloodline of those before us to us and then to those after us. If we are unaware of the genetics, it may not be nonexistent.

As I navigated those turbulent waters of grief and confusion, my faith in God guided me toward the transformation I needed. In times of distress, our faith is called into action. When things are going well, we do not need to believe that things will improve as they are already doing well. However, when things get out of control, then we get a fuller understanding of the fact that *"Now faith is confidence in what we hope for and assurance about what we do not see." (Hebrews 11:1 – NIV).*

UNDERSTANDING AND PROCESSING THE INITIAL SHOCK AND GRIEF

My fears were realized upon receiving this diagnosis. I had seen the signs and decided I would face the situation head-on. However, I was not prepared. I thought I would be, but I was not. It started with a heaviness that went down to the pit of my stomach and progressed to disbelief and denial. My core was rattled, and I struggled to find my footing in this new reality.

Mourning the future I had envisioned for my child, a future free from the challenges that this diagnosis now presented, I grieved a loss I had never imagined. Consequently, tears became my silent companion whenever I had moments alone. It was an uncharted territory for me, a journey I had not signed up for, and there I was, grappling with emotions that threatened to consume me.

I had entered a process of grieving I never anticipated. Grieving entails several stages, and for those of us who experience grief, it is important that we go through the grieving process. It is equally important for us to be present in the moment and experience the pain and sense of loss. Do not try to hide the pain behind an addiction, as then we will only be adding another issue to what we are currently facing. Also, imagine not going through the experience and feeling the emotions. How will we learn and adapt for our family in the future, and how will we help others facing the same situation?

STAGES OF GRIEF

Elisabeth Kübler-Ross, a pioneering figure in the field of grief and loss, introduced the well-known five stages of grief model through her 1969 book, "On Death and Dying." Initially, she developed this model to help individuals with terminal illnesses cope with the impending reality of their own death. However, the model quickly found a broader application in understanding the broader spectrum of grief experiences.

Kübler-Ross' model outlines the five stages: denial, anger, bargaining, depression, and acceptance. While these stages are often discussed as a linear progression, with people moving from one stage to the next, it is important to note that Kübler-Ross herself emphasized that these stages are not strictly sequential. The process of grief is deeply personal and non-linear, as individuals may experience these stages in varying orders or even skip some altogether.

In essence, not everyone will go through every stage, and the way grief unfolds can differ significantly from one loss to another. Each bereavement is a unique emotional journey influenced by the individual's personal experiences, relationships, and coping mechanisms. Kübler-Ross' model remains a valuable framework for understanding grief. Still, it should be viewed as a guide rather than a rigid roadmap, allowing room for the complexity and individuality of the grieving process.

Similarly, not every parent or caregiver of children with special needs will feel the same or have the same experiences. It is important to note that everyone's feelings and journey are valid despite the differences.

SHIFTING PERSPECTIVES: EMBRACING YOUR CHILD'S UNIQUE JOURNEY

A few months before getting pregnant, I went into the bookstore and saw a book by James Dobson titled **Building Confidence In Your Child,** and for some reason, I bought the book as I thought it would be a good book. I read it while pregnant, not knowing that the truths I uncovered within those pages would be instrumental in navigating my parenting journey years later.

Time has a beautiful way of bringing moments and experiences together, creating a beautiful mosaic we never thought possible. Our perception changes, and we experience transformation we never anticipated. In the midst of the waves of grief, I came to a realization, like an epiphany, that would forever alter my outlook. Shifting my perspective was not just an option but was the lifeline to survival.

My mantra, embracing my child for all he is and helping him thrive, came back to my memory. This is a point I had settled on since I was pregnant and read Dr. James Dobsons' book, *Building Confidence in Your Child.* I then decided within myself that my son was not defined by his diagnosis; he was defined by the boundless potential placed within him by the Creator. The world may label him, but I chose to see him as an individual brimming with strengths and talents waiting to be nurtured.

FOSTERING SELF-COMPASSION AND ACCEPTANCE

Self-compassion is simply turning the kindness and understanding we extend to others inward. On the exciting journey of raising children with special needs, we must cultivate self-compassion. Discovering the wellspring of self-compassion within and tapping into it will be our saving grace in many instances. You see, our society is one that, in many instances, accuses parents of bad parenting when our children with special needs act out, for example, when they are overstimulated or cannot fit within the rigidity of sitting in one place for extended periods. When those harsh comments are made towards us, we must extend kindness and understanding to ourselves, knowing we are doing our best.

Acknowledging our feelings is paramount. It is okay to feel a kaleidoscope of emotions, to experience moments of frustration, anger, and sorrow. We must grant ourselves permission to experience these emotions and heal at our own pace. The aim here is not to achieve perfection but to make progress. The same situations that get us agitated today should not be the same situations that get us agitated a few months from now.

Acceptance emerged steadily, teaching me that acknowledging my child's needs did not negate his potential. It is a delicate dance between acknowledging reality and refusing to be defined by it. Each child has their own strengths and weaknesses and will be placed at different areas of the special needs spectrum. Some will be high functioning, meaning they are brilliant in many ways and able to do well either in academics or an area of interest. At the same time, this may not be so for others; whichever situation we find ourselves in, it is important to accept our realities and not look at our friends or family. For indeed, comparison is the thief of joy.

A PERSONAL JOURNEY: FROM GRIEF TO EMBRACE

For years, I carried the weight of my emotions in silence. The diagnosis became an unspoken secret, a chapter of my life that I was hesitant to share. It was a heavy burden to bear alone, and the isolation compounded the pain. However, a transformative moment arrived, one that would forever alter the trajectory of my journey.

The game-changer for me was a shift in perspective that transformed grief into an embrace and fear into empowerment. It was a conscious decision to shift from mourning the loss of a preconceived notion to celebrating the unique and beautiful being my child was becoming. Instead of focusing on what my child might not achieve, I reveled in his ability to think outside the box, creativity, and boundless innovation.

The realization that my son's journey was extraordinary in its own right filled me with an indescribable sense of pride. I began to share our story, to speak openly about his diagnosis, and to shed the cloak of isolation that had shrouded me for so long. With each word spoken, I chiseled away at the stigma surrounding special needs, replacing it with a narrative of strength, resilience, and limitless potential.

NAVIGATING THE SPECTRUM OF EMOTIONS

As parents and caregivers, we must permit ourselves to traverse the spectrum of emotions. Grief is not a destination; it is a passage that eventually leads to a place of acceptance, understanding, and growth. It is natural to mourn the loss of what we had envisioned, but it is equally essential to celebrate the possibilities that lie ahead.

In the chapters that follow, we will explore strategies to navigate this intricate spectrum of emotions. We will delve into the art of self-compassion, the power of community, and the transformative effects of embracing our child's unique journey. Together, we will learn that within the depths of grief, we find the wellspring of love and resilience that empowers us to stand tall, face the unknown, and embrace the extraordinary journey that awaits us.

REFLECTIONS

How did you feel learning of your child's diagnosis?

_____

_____

_____

_____

_____

How do you feel today?

_____

_____

_____

_____

What would self-compassion look like for you?

_____

_____

_____

_____

How would acceptance improve your parenting for your special needs child(ren)?

_____

_____

_____

_____

_____

AFFIRMATIONS

1. I am equipped to parent my child regardless of a special needs diagnosis.
2. I practice the delicate dance between acknowledging my reality and refusing to be defined by it.
3. My child is filled with boundless potential placed within him/her by the Creator.

THOUGHTS TO PONDER

"For I know the plans I have for you," declares the Lord, "plans to prosper you and not to harm you, plans to give you hope and a future." (Jeremiah 29:11 – NIV).

"We must let go of the life we have planned, so as to accept the one that is waiting for us." —Joseph Campbell

NOTE TO SELF

_____

_____

_____

_____

_____

_____

SELF-CARE CORNER - SELF TALK

In the intricacies of life, I have found myself journeying through a vast spectrum of emotions. Like the ocean's changing tides, my feelings ebb and flow, which is perfectly okay. I have learned that the weight of my emotions need not be a burden but a testament to my humanity.

I have shifted my perspective. I have made a conscious choice to trade grief for embrace and fear for empowerment. I now know that grief is not an endpoint but a bridge that leads to understanding and growth. There were moments of heaviness, disbelief, and even tears, but they were stepping stones on my path to a deeper connection with my child's unique journey.

I have chosen to release preconceived notions and celebrate the boundless potential within my child and myself. I am not defined by diagnoses or societal expectations but by the limitless beauty that resides within. I have uncovered an unwavering wellspring of love and resilience in embracing this truth, guiding me through the uncharted terrain.

I have the power to nurture self-compassion and understanding. I grant myself the permission to acknowledge my feelings and heal at my own pace. Within the depths of my emotions, I find the strength to stand tall and celebrate the unique journey that is mine to embrace. So, with each step, I will remind myself that my emotions are a testament to my strength and this journey is one of love, resilience, and endless potential.

CHAPTER 2

CULTIVATING A POSITIVE ATTITUDE

Mindset can be viewed as the established set of attitudes held by someone. It is no wonder mindset is so crucial as we are all products of our attitudes. Our attitudes determine our habits, and our habits determine our todays and tomorrows. Hence, if we want a different tomorrow, we must work to make the necessary changes to our attitudes today. It then becomes evident that our mindset influences our thoughts, beliefs, and attitudes, which directly affects our reality. For parents and caregivers of children with special needs, cultivating a positive mindset becomes not just a choice but a necessity—an unwavering force that shapes our perception, fuels our actions, and influences the very development of our precious young ones.

According to Schramayr (2018), when someone faces a condition affecting part of their body, it is common for them to reduce their involvement in all activities and focus on those things they can not do. Schramayr (2018) was sure to highlight that a simple shift in a person's mindset can cause them to learn to thrive in new ways and adapt to their new challenges. Likewise, it is for us parents and caregivers of children with special needs. It is quite easy for us to reduce all our activities and instead focus on things we cannot do or things that the new diagnosis will negatively impact. But there are so many things that our dear children can still do and do well. Let us, therefore, embrace the possibilities.

THE POWER OF MINDSET IN SUPPORTING YOUR CHILD'S DEVELOPMENT

A child's journey through life is profoundly influenced by the mindset we, as parents and caregivers, bring to the table. Our attitude serves as a compass, guiding us through uncharted territories and steering our children towards their full potential. A positive mindset is not a mere platitude; it is a catalyst for growth, a beacon of hope that empowers us to recognize and nurture our children's unique gifts and abilities.

When we embrace a growth mindset, we pave the way for our child's development. We see challenges as opportunities for growth, setbacks as stepping stones toward success, and obstacles as invitations to unlock untapped potential. By fostering a mindset that believes in possibilities, we inspire our children to reach for the stars, to defy limits, and to set their own course despite the odds.

There are two main types of mindset: the growth mindset and the fixed mindset. A growth mindset, in its most basic form, is an attitude that fosters lifelong learning. This attitude takes the position that one can grow and develop into the person they desire to become with hard work and dedication. It is an attitude that embraces the process of change and growth. On the other hand, a fixed mindset is just the opposite. It is an attitude that believes that talents and abilities are unchangeable. But what does this have to do with parenting?

Our mindset influences the way we parent and care for our children. According to Aunola et al., 1999, parents who actively cultivate a growth mindset are more likely to parent their children using autonomy-supportive methods. In doing so, they encourage their children to explore and learn. This type of autonomy-supportive parenting style is linked to what is called mastery-oriented parenting, where learning and the process of learning take precedence, resulting in positive outcomes.

Let us break it down: there is autonomy-supportive and controlling parenting. Autonomy-supportive parenting involves encouraging children to explore their environment and practice independent problem-solving and decision-making. Controlling-parenting involves a tight regulation of children's behaviour, with commands being issued and external incentives.

Another dimension of parenting involves the extent to which parents display mastery- and performance-oriented parenting. Mastery-oriented parenting entails encouraging our children to value the learning process and the importance of the effort put in. Performance-oriented parenting is more focused on achieving high levels of performance with little effort.

This is valuable information for many of us as parents and caregivers of children with special needs. Many of our children with special needs can become independent individuals. As for these children, it is important that we train them in such a way that they can become independent and develop their skills to become global citizens. Sometimes, as parents and caregivers, we try to shield them from what we think will not be in their best interest, and honestly speaking, the only caution with that is for us not to attempt to shield our children so much that they are limited. In other words, let us not allow our protection to handicap our children.

Let's think of the eagle; when it is time for the eaglet to learn to fly, the mother eagle pushes the eaglet off a cliff in an effort to force the young bird to learn to fly. Though we have no need to push our young one off a cliff, the principle of the eagle holds true. We must be attentive to the growth and development of our young ones and allow them to grow and learn new skills. We must not allow ourselves to become hindrances to our children but more of a springboard from which they launch.

OVERCOMING SELF-LIMITING BELIEFS AND SOCIETAL PRESSURES

Nurturing a child with special needs can be filled with self-doubt and societal pressures. It is quite easy to fall prey to these self-limiting beliefs, internalize misconceptions, and allow our confidence to erode. Yet, we must recognize that these beliefs are not truths; they are views constructed to confine our vision and shackle our aspirations.

In the realm of special needs, societal pressures can be daunting adversaries. The judgments of others, the weight of comparisons, and the echo of well-intentioned yet misinformed advice can resound through our thoughts. However, a positive mindset empowers us to rise above these pressures, to shatter the shackles of conformity, and to carve a unique path that celebrates our child's individuality.

Here, we learn one of the most valuable practices: knowing the truth. It becomes an urgency for us to arm ourselves with knowledge. Therefore, as parents and caregivers, it is important for us to learn about our child's diagnosis and do our research. In this modern day, when we have easy access to information with a simple device called a phone, we have no excuse to stay misinformed.

We will not understand everything overnight, and it will take reading or listening to several resources before we have a full picture of our realities. Nevertheless, it is something we must do. Knowing the facts about the diagnosis, knowing our children, and reframing that information along biblical principles, such as we are made in the image of God (see Genesis 1:27), puts us in a place of expertise with regard to our children and their respective diagnoses. We learn to understand that most will not understand our journey and will give misinformation and pass judgment. But guess what? It is their misunderstanding, misinformed position, and wrong judgment, not yours. Now, if someone is willing to learn, you can take the opportunity to share accurate information. However, if they are not, we as parents must be comfortable with being misjudged, knowing we are doing the right thing and not allowing others to get into our heads.

I am in no way suggesting that it is easy, but our realities require us to develop mental fortitude. Knowing that judgment is passed incorrectly and not allowing it to discourage us is a skill we must develop. One way we can do so is to remind ourselves of the truth and the facts; truths such as we are made in the image of God and His likeness. God Himself is our vindicator.

CULTIVATING RESILIENCE AND ADAPTABILITY

Resilience can be thought of as simply our ability to withstand challenges or "bounce back' from misfortunes. Words that can be used in the place of resilience are toughness and elasticity. Adaptability speaks to our ability to adjust to new circumstances. These two character traits become increasingly important as the path we find ourselves as parents and caregivers of neurodivergent or special needs children is not linear.

The journey we embark upon is not a straight path; it is one filled with twists and turns, highs and lows, challenges and triumphs. Resilience becomes our armor, our shield against the storms that may rage. The inner fortitude allows us to bounce back from adversity, weather the fiercest of tempests, and emerge stronger on the other side.

A positive mindset is the catalyst for cultivating resilience—an resolute belief that no matter the obstacle, we possess the capacity to navigate through it. Resilience is not the absence of difficulty; it is the ability to harness our inner strength, to lean on our support networks, and to adapt in the face of adversity. In cultivating resilience, we model for our children the power of tenacity, the art of perseverance, and the beauty of resilience in the face of uncertainty.

Our adaptability impacts the extent to which we are able to be resilient. Our ability to adjust to changing situations with the aim to do our best and be our best will determine our resilience in this dynamic season of our lives.

SHAPING MINDSET: PRACTICAL STRATEGIES FOR POSITIVE ATTITUDE

1. **Mindful Reflection:** Dedicate time each day for self-reflection. Embrace moments of stillness to examine

your thoughts and emotions, and consciously choose to redirect negative ones towards positive ones.

2. **Affirmations:** Introduce positive affirmations into your daily routine. These powerful declarations can reshape your beliefs and instill confidence in yourself and your child.

3. **Seeking Support:** Connect with fellow parents, caregivers, family, friends and teachers. Sharing experiences, challenges, and successes can inspire a collective mindset of growth and possibility.

4. **Educational Resources:** Immerse yourself in educational materials that emphasize the importance of mindset. Expanding your knowledge empowers you to impart these invaluable lessons to your child.

5. **Modeling Positivity:** Children are keen observers. Your own attitude and reactions influence their mindset. Lead by example, showing them how to face challenges with optimism and a solution-focused approach.

REFLECTIONS

Are there any mindsets or beliefs that need adjusting? If so, what are they?

_____

_____

_____

_____

_____

Have any self-limiting beliefs or societal pressures influenced the way you parent/care for your children?

_____

_____

_____

_____

_____

_____

How can resilience and adaptability be cultivated in your parenting approach?

_____

_____

_____

_____

_____

Identify the practices that will be cultivated to develop a positive mindset in yourself as the parent or caregiver.

_____

_____

_____

_____

_____

How will you encourage your child(ren) to develop resilience and adaptability?

_____

_____

_____

_____

_____

AFFIRMATIONS

1. I am equipped to parent my child regardless of a special needs diagnosis.
2. I practice cultivating a positive mindset.
3. I create a positive space/home for my child to grow and develop into all he/she was created to be.

THOUGHTS TO PONDER

"Finally, brothers and sisters, whatever is true, whatever is noble, whatever is right, whatever is pure, whatever is lovely, whatever is admirable—if anything is excellent or

praiseworthy—think about such things." (Philippians 4:8 - NIV).

"Once your mindset changes, everything on the outside will change along with it." —Steve Maraboli

NOTE TO SELF

_____

_____

_____

_____

_____

SELF-CARE CORNER - A POEM

In the grand tapestry of life, we weave our way.
Through twists and turns, we greet each brand-new day.
Our mindset, like a beacon, guides us on this quest,
A positive attitude, in our hearts, we manifest.

Resilience is our armor, as challenges come our way,
With adaptability by our side, we're ready to sway.
In mindful reflection, we find our inner light,
Affirmations empower us, shining through the night.

With support and knowledge, we stand strong and tall,
Leading by example, we rise above it all.
On this delicate journey, we dare to tread,
A positive mindset, our children we shall lead.

CHAPTER 3

HOLISTIC APPROACH TO BUILDING A STRONG FOUNDATION

When we contemplate the magnificence of the world's iconic structures—the Taj Mahal, the Chrysler Building, or the Neuschwanstein Castle—a fundamental truth comes to light: the foundation stands as the bedrock of their grandeur. Indeed, the essence of any edifice lies in its foundation. The taller and more intricate a structure we envision, the more critical the solidity of the foundation becomes. It is a simple principle: if we seek to elevate, we must first delve deeper.

Similarly, for parents and caregivers of children with special needs, building a strong foundation stands as a cornerstone—a foundation that embraces not only the physical aspects but also includes the emotional, mental, and social well-being of both the child and the dedicated individuals supporting them. This holistic approach sets the stage for a journey that isn't just navigable but also enriching, rewarding, and remarkably resilient. This analogy, resonating deeply with our hearts, extends to the realm of caring for our beautiful, special needs children. Each child holds within them a unique blend of needs and capabilities, strengths and weaknesses that make them truly exceptional. Understanding one child with special needs is merely the beginning, for their needs are as diverse and distinctive as the stars in the night sky.

Some of our cherished children face physical disabilities, navigating a world that demands assistive technologies like canes and braille for those with visual impairments. It is a visible challenge, met with visible solutions—technology and compassion intertwining to illuminate their path. Conversely, there are those whose needs lie beneath the surface, hidden from the naked eye. Children grappling with ADHD, for instance, call for support to help channel and sustain their focus in a world often bustling with distractions.

In this delicate interplay of diverse needs, we find the essence of our approach: building strong foundations for these extraordinary individuals. Our quest is to immerse ourselves into the depths of understanding, to listen to their stories, and to grasp the nuances of their unique journeys. Through this understanding, we construct the foundation upon which their growth, potential, and happiness rest. Our warmth, dedication, and steadfast love converge to create a safe, nurturing space—a bedrock that nurtures their development and empowers them to flourish.

NURTURING PHYSICAL WELL-BEING: NUTRITION, EXERCISE, AND HEALTHCARE

A child's physical well-being stands as the cornerstone upon which their entire development is built. In the embrace of proper nutrition, the joy of exercise, and the security of healthcare, we find the elements crucial to nurturing their growing bodies and blossoming spirits. As caregivers, it is our profound responsibility to lay the groundwork for a healthy lifestyle that supports physical growth and nourishes emotional well-being.

Nutrition - A balanced and nutritious diet takes on heightened importance when caring for children with special needs. The foods we choose for our children significantly impact their energy levels, cognitive function, and overall health. A diet rich in whole foods, lean proteins, fruits, and vegetables nourishes the body and supports brain development and immune function. It is a conscious choice, an act of love that sets the stage for a vibrant life.

Understanding the specific nutritional needs of our children is paramount. For each child, these needs may vary, necessitating a tailored approach. In my personal experience, I have found organic foods to be best, emphasizing their purity and lack of harmful chemicals. I would wholeheartedly suggest incorporating organic options into your child's diet whenever possible.

The Eatwell Guide provides a roadmap, dividing the foods and drinks we consume into five main groups: fruit and vegetables, starchy carbohydrates, proteins, dairy and alternatives, and oils and spreads. Variety is the key—choosing a diverse range of foods from each group ensures a well-rounded nutrient intake. Creativity becomes a vital tool in encouraging a balanced diet for our kids, especially the picky eaters. It is important to remain patient and persistent, continually offering various foods. Someday, unexpectedly, they may try and even like something new.

Exercise - Physical activity is not merely a pastime but a vehicle for physical and emotional growth. Tailoring exercises to suit your child's abilities fosters motor skills, strengthens muscles, and boosts self-confidence. Swimming, yoga, outdoor play, or any activity that aligns with your child's preferences can be incorporated into their daily routines.

Beyond the physical benefits, exercise contributes significantly to cognitive and emotional development. The joy of movement and play is essential for every child, offering a sense of accomplishment and happiness. Consult with your healthcare provider to determine the best exercise routine for your child, considering their unique needs and abilities.

Healthcare - A comprehensive healthcare regimen is foundational for a child's overall well-being. Regular medical check-ups, therapy sessions, and screenings are essential pillars in ensuring potential health issues are identified and addressed promptly. Co-morbidities or other illnesses can often accompany special needs, making these regular check-ups all the more crucial.

Based on the guidance of experienced medical professionals, early intervention can make a world of difference. Through these early interventions, we navigate challenges and embrace a path of continuous progress and growth. Partnering with healthcare providers who deeply understand your child's unique needs and circumstances is an invaluable step toward ensuring their long-term health and development.

In this collective endeavor of nourishing physical well-being through nutrition, exercise, and healthcare, we lay the foundation for a future where our children can thrive and embrace life's endless possibilities. Let us approach this journey with a warm and caring spirit, guided by love and dedication, for the benefit of our cherished children and the richness they bring to our world.

Prioritizing Our Own Well-Being - As we focus on nourishing and nurturing our precious children, we must remember that our well-being is equally significant. As parents and caregivers, we are the steady compass guiding our children through the ups and downs of life. Just as we diligently provide our children with proper nutrition, encourage exercise, and follow up with medical check-ups, we must extend the same care to ourselves. We stand as the pillars of strength and love for our special needs children and must prioritize our health. In truth, by practicing good nutrition, engaging in regular exercise, and maintaining a diligent approach to our medical care, we enhance our quality of life and ensure that we are here to support and love our children for the long and beautiful journey ahead. After all, it is through our well-being and love that we can best care for our beloved children.

PRIORITIZING MENTAL HEALTH: COPING STRATEGIES

Mental health, a delicate balance of emotional, psychological, and social well-being, profoundly influences our cognition, perception, and behavior. Fusar-Poli et al. (2020) beautifully define good mental health as a state of well-being that empowers individuals to cope with the ebb and flow of life's stresses, enabling them to function productively. Emotional health encompasses our ability to navigate both positive and negative emotions with awareness. Psychological health embodies the sum of our thoughts, feelings, relationships, and daily existence.

On the other hand, social well-being encompasses cultivating and sustaining healthy relationships, valuing diversity, and fostering a sense of belonging through open communication and mutual respect.

The journey of caring for a child with special needs unfolds through a terrain of triumphs and challenges, joys and moments of vulnerability. As parents and caregivers, our emotional and mental well-being is delicately woven with our children's. Prioritizing our own emotional health equips us to provide the support our children need. Through our actions and practices that prioritize emotional well-being, we model for our children how to cultivate good mental health, even in the face of changes or adversity.

Coping Strategies - Caregivers often carry the weight of immense responsibilities, making it crucial to recognize the importance of self-care. Engaging in activities that bring joy, seeking support through therapy or support groups, and practicing mindfulness can help alleviate stress and enhance emotional resilience. By tending to our emotional well-being, we create an environment of stability that positively influences our child's emotional development.

In this journey of nurturing, we can also guide our young ones in developing coping skills through visual representations, like pictures, to help them identify and express their emotions. Role play is another powerful tool that allows us to demonstrate coping mechanisms and navigate different situations with our children. Reflection, a practice that promotes self-awareness and growth, can be initiated through simple conversations with verbal children or through other forms of communication for non-verbal children.

Emotional Regulation - Our children look to us for guidance in managing their emotions. By modeling healthy emotional regulation and communication, we equip our children with the tools to navigate their feelings and interactions gracefully. Creating a safe space for open dialogue and emotional expression lays a solid foundation for your child's emotional growth.

When addressing emotional regulation, we can employ simple yet effective steps to guide our children. By helping them learn about their emotional levels and the situations that trigger intense emotions, we empower them to understand and manage their emotional responses. Emotion-level charts serve as valuable tools for this purpose. Describing various ways children can react and respond to their emotions allows them to develop a nuanced understanding of their emotional landscape. Practicing calm-down activities together, such as taking deep breaths or counting, offers invaluable coping mechanisms they can carry with them throughout their lives.

As parents and caregivers, let us embrace the importance of nurturing our mental health and well-being as a foundation upon which we provide the best care and support for our special needs children. Through love, understanding, and resilience, we can create a harmonious environment where both our children and ourselves can flourish, navigating life's beauty together. Remember, by prioritizing our own well-being, we ensure we are present and thriving, ready to embrace each precious moment with our beloved children.

ESTABLISHING A SUPPORTIVE NETWORK: GOD, FAMILY, FRIENDS, AND COMMUNITY

The journey of raising a child with special needs is an extraordinary expedition, not meant to be undertaken in solitude. The heart of this voyage lies in building a robust support network of family, friends, and community that fortifies the foundation of care, understanding, and shared experiences. It is essential to understand and appreciate that each person's support will vary; some will be able to give more support compared to others. However, it is crucial not to allow oneself to become distracted or succumb to negative emotions, for this journey is a unique and beautiful one, deserving of celebration and collective strength.

God - "Children are a heritage from the Lord, offspring a reward from him." (Psalm 127:3 - NIV). When that heritage is shared with us, it is wise for us to partner with Him. The Sovereign God and Creator saw it fit to share his heritage with us because He entrusted them into our care. Our children are actually a reward from Him. Yes, I know some days feel overwhelming, but God is ready and waiting to partner with us in raising our children. He said we should cast our cares on Him (see Psalm 55:22). For me, my biggest cares are my children. I have had to pray a prayer like this very often: *"Lord, Your Word says we should cast our cares upon You because You care for us. Abba, my greatest care are my children. I commit them into Your hands."* Yet, there are times when we simply don't know what to do. He is the all-knowing God, and His Word declares, *"If any of you lacks wisdom, you should ask God, who gives generously to all without finding fault, and it will be given to you." (James 1:5 - NIV).* Personally, partnering with God in raising my children, particularly my special needs child, has been the most life-changing decision for my parenting journey, and it has yielded the most fruit.

Family - Family forms the bedrock of support. Open communication and collaboration ensure that everyone is on the same page when it comes to the child's needs, goals, and well-being. Siblings, too, play a crucial role in shaping the child's development, and fostering a sense of unity within the family helps build a resilient and nurturing environment.

Friends and Peers - The friendships formed between your child and their peers provide opportunities for growth, socialization, and mutual learning. Encouraging inclusive interactions and facilitating friendships nurtures a sense of belonging and expands your child's horizons.

Community - The broader community can be a wellspring of support and resources. Local organizations, support groups, and online communities connect you with like-minded individuals who share similar experiences. Participating in community activities provides a sense of belonging and enriches your child's social interactions.

A HOLISTIC LEGACY: BUILDING STRONG FOUNDATIONS

Building a strong foundation is not a singular task on the journey of nurturing a child with special needs; it is an ongoing commitment that intertwines the threads of physical health, emotional well-being, and social connection. By embracing a holistic approach, we create an environment that empowers our children to thrive, regardless of their challenges.

REFLECTIONS

How intentional are you at developing strong foundations for both yourself and your special needs child(ren)?

_____

_____

_____

_____

_____

Identify ways in which you can improve on nurturing your physical well-being as well as that of your special needs child(ren). Could it be something that can be done together?

_____

_____

_____

_____

_____

How will you establish a supportive network or improve upon your existing network?

_____

_____

_____

_____

_____

How will you prioritize your mental well-being as well as that of your child(ren)?

_____

_____

_____

_____

_____

What is your greatest takeaway from this chapter?

_____

_____

_____

_____

_____

AFFIRMATIONS

1. I am an empowered caregiver, nurturing the unique potential within my special needs child.
2. I cultivate a loving and supportive network that uplifts and sustains me on this journey.
3. I embrace self-care as a vital component of my caregiving role, nurturing my well-being to nurture others.

Write one affirmation for yourself based on what you have read and meditated on.

_____

_____

_____

_____

_____

THOUGHTS TO PONDER

"They are like a man building a house, who dug down deep and laid the foundation on rock. When a flood came, the torrent struck that house but could not shake it, because it was well built." (Luke 6:48 – NIV).

"You can't build a great building on a weak foundation. You must have a solid foundation if you're going to have a strong superstructure." —Gordon B Hinckley

NOTE TO SELF

_____

_____

_____

_____

_____

SELF-CARE CORNER - A SHORT STORY

LUCY'S HAVEN

The Turner family resided in a charming cottage in a small countryside community, where rolling hills and meadows stretched as far as the eye could see. Life in this tranquil corner of the world was serene, a place where nature's beauty met the warmth of a tight-knit community. Here, the Turners nurtured their extraordinary love and raised their exceptional child, Lucy.

Lucy was born deaf and later diagnosed with dyslexia, but her family embraced their unique journey. The countryside offered a backdrop of rustic beauty and a natural haven for their holistic approach. Under the vast, open skies, the Turners partnered with the grace of God, finding solace and wisdom in their faith.

Lucy's father, Samuel, was a farmer, and he understood the importance of nurturing her physical well-being. He cultivated an organic garden where the family harvested fresh, wholesome vegetables. Samuel and Lucy often took leisurely walks through the fields, embracing the countryside's bounty and the healing power of nature.

In their cozy home, Lucy's mother, Eliza, made it a point to prioritize her daughter's emotional and mental health. Their home was adorned with arts and crafts, each reflecting their inner joy and resilience. Coping strategies became integral to their daily life, and they navigated challenges with heartfelt love.

The countryside was a sanctuary for the Turners and a community that stood as a pillar of support. Neighbours and friends, like the gentle rustling of leaves in the wind, celebrated Lucy's uniqueness. They gathered in farmhouses, hosted picnics by the river, and ensured that Lucy's friendships blossomed, embracing the values of inclusivity.

In the heart of the countryside community, Lucy thrived. She found her strength not in her special needs but in the love that surrounded her. The Turners were building a legacy of resilience, love, and harmony, honoring the whole child. Their countryside haven empowered Lucy to reach for the stars, to defy limits, and to set her own course in life.

CHAPTER 4

CONNECTING WITH YOUR CHILD

In high school, I was introduced to a simple yet profound definition of communication: it is the means of sending and receiving information. This definition, still as relevant today as it was then, underscores the fundamental essence of human interaction. I also learned that anything that disrupts the communication process is termed "noise." It struck me that sometimes, what the person receiving the information understands may not align with the sender's original intent. From this simple model, I grasped the deep importance of communication in our lives.

In the case of our special needs children, communication is no less significant. However, the process can be influenced by a myriad of additional factors, much like the "noise" in the communication model. Consider the diagnosis itself, a significant presence that can influence how our children perceive and interact with the world. The range of communication capabilities among special needs children is vast; some are verbal, while others are not. Even those able to communicate verbally, some may struggle to understand social cues or have difficulty reading emotions. The complexities of these unique experiences require us, as caregivers and parents, to explore and adapt our communication approach to foster understanding and connection.

Communication is essential to human relationships, and it serves as the delicate thread that weaves hearts together. It transcends mere words, creating bonds that resonate deeply and offer the promise of connection. When raising a child with special needs, communication takes on an even more profound role—it becomes a bridge. This bridge links their world with ours, allowing for a nuanced understanding, empathy, and, most importantly, a sense of belonging. Empowering communication in this context goes beyond the mere conveyance of information; it is the key to unlocking the potential for growth and meaningful connections that transcend barriers. As parents and caregivers, our approach to communication is vital in nurturing our children's development and enriching their lives.

UNDERSTANDING AND NURTURING COMMUNICATION

Understanding the unique communication needs of special needs children is the first step toward empowering effective and empathetic communication. It begins by acknowledging that diverse and often delicate factors may shape the world of communication for these children. As caregivers, we must adapt and cater to the individual communication styles of our children, whether they are non-verbal, struggle with social cues, or face other challenges.

One of the core principles of nurturing communication is active listening. It is not just about hearing words but about truly comprehending the feelings, thoughts, and emotions behind those words. This might involve alternative forms of expression for non-verbal children, such as gestures, pictures, or assistive technology.

Another essential aspect is patience. Communication might take time, especially when understanding and expressing emotions. It is about allowing your child the space and freedom to communicate in their own way and at their own pace, without pressure or frustration.

Empathy plays a crucial role as well. By placing ourselves in our child's shoes, we can better understand their perspective and adapt our communication accordingly. This empathetic approach fosters a sense of trust and security in the child, enhancing the quality of the connection.

In our journey of empowering communication, creating an inclusive environment is crucial. This entails not only fostering understanding within the family but also in the broader community. It is about educating others on the unique communication needs of special needs children, promoting patience, and dispelling misconceptions. By raising awareness and advocating for inclusive spaces, we enable our children to interact and communicate with the world around them more freely and with greater ease. Communication is indeed a bridge—one that, when built with love, empathy, and understanding, unites our worlds and makes our lives all the more beautiful.

EFFECTIVE COMMUNICATION TECHNIQUES FOR CHILDREN WITH DIVERSE NEEDS

Every child is a unique blend of strengths, challenges, and individual communication styles. Tailoring your approach to match your child's specific needs is fundamental to fostering effective communication. For children with diverse needs, communication can take countless forms, from verbal language to nonverbal cues, augmentative and alternative communication (AAC) devices to sign language. Understanding and adapting to these varied modes of expression enable you to connect with your child on their terms.

Communication is a universal human experience, transcending borders, languages, and abilities. It is the thread that binds us to one another, allowing us to share our thoughts, emotions, and desires. In the case of children with diverse needs, communication takes on an even more profound role—it is the gateway to unlocking their unique potential, building connections, and nurturing their sense of self.

Communication is a dialogue, and it is essential to remember that even if our children cannot respond verbally, they are still listening, processing, and experiencing the world around them. As caregivers, we are responsible for creating an environment of open communication and inviting our children to participate in this ongoing dialogue.

Talk to your children about both the serious and fun matters of life and everything in between. Encourage them to respond in any way they can, whether it is a smile, a raised eyebrow, or another nonverbal cue. The aim is to build communication skills within our children, expand their understanding of the world, and offer them the opportunity to engage in vibrant human interaction.

Visual Supports – These may be viewed as a tangible language. Visual supports, such as picture cards, schedules, and visual timetables, provide children with a tangible way to comprehend and communicate. These supports enhance predictability, reduce anxiety, and effectively empower children to express their needs and preferences.

Visual supports also prove invaluable when establishing routines for our young ones. By presenting a visual routine, children gain an overview of what is to be done and the order in which activities will unfold. Picture cards can be used to help children identify their feelings or to convey a story. The uses are diverse, limited only by our creativity and the unique needs of our children.

AAC Devices and Technology grants our children a voice. Augmentative and Alternative Communication (AAC) devices encompass an array of tools and technologies, each offering a bridge to self-expression for nonverbal children. Gestures, communication boards, pictures, symbols, and drawings are common AAC tools. They may range from low-tech, like a simple laminated page of pictures, to sophisticated, such as digitized speech output devices.

These tools open doors to self-expression for children who may have difficulty with verbal communication. They enable children to convey their thoughts, emotions, and desires, granting them a voice in the world. The range of options within AAC devices ensures that there is a solution tailored to each child's unique needs.

Sign Language and Gestures is a universal language that transcends verbal limitations. For some children, this form of communication is incredibly effective and meaningful. Learning and using these forms of expression fosters a unique and powerful connection.

FOSTERING CONNECTION THROUGH ACTIVE LISTENING AND EMPATHY

Communication is not just about speaking; it is a balance of speaking and listening. Active listening is the cornerstone of meaningful communication. It requires more than just hearing words; it involves immersing ourselves in the moment and attuning to the nuances of body language, tone, and emotion.

When we practice active listening, we communicate our respect, presence, and willingness to engage authentically. We show our children that their verbal or nonverbal words matter and that they are valued participants in our shared dialogue.

Empathy, the bridge that connects hearts, is equally vital. When we step into our child's shoes, we create a deep understanding that transcends words. Empathy acknowledges their challenges, validates their emotions, and fosters an environment of trust and open communication. It demonstrates our commitment to standing beside them and supporting their unique journey.

ENCOURAGING SELF-EXPRESSION AND SELF-ADVOCACY

Empowering communication extends far beyond the act of conveying thoughts; it encompasses the vital aspects of self-expression and self-advocacy. As caregivers, our role goes beyond teaching children to express their ideas—it includes equipping them with the tools to navigate their world, assert their needs, and advocate for their rights.

Self-Expression - Creating an environment that values and encourages self-expression is the foundation upon which confident communication is built. Self-expression can take on various forms for children with diverse needs, and it is our responsibility to nurture these avenues.

Art, music, and play are powerful tools for self-expression. They provide children with a means to communicate in ways that feel most natural and comfortable to them. Encouraging artistic exploration allows them to convey thoughts, emotions, and stories when words may not suffice. Music can be a universal language where melodies and rhythms become a medium for expression. Through play, children immerse themselves in imaginative worlds where they can communicate their innermost thoughts and feelings.

As caregivers, we play a pivotal role in creating an environment where self-expression is celebrated and encouraged. By offering diverse avenues for creative expression, we allow our children to develop a strong sense of self and confidence in sharing their thoughts and emotions.

Self-Advocacy - As children grow, they must acquire the ability to advocate for themselves. This crucial life skill fosters independence and self-confidence, enabling them to navigate a world that may not always understand their unique needs.

Teaching children to assert their preferences, needs, and boundaries is a transformative process. Role-playing scenarios and providing guidance empower children to become effective self-advocates. By practicing real-life situations and discussing potential responses, children learn to communicate their needs and preferences assertively.

Empowering children to be their own advocates is about helping them in the present and preparing them for the future. It instills a strong sense of self-worth and confidence, enabling them to navigate diverse environments, advocate for necessary accommodations, and become active participants in their own lives.

NURTURING EMPOWERED COMMUNICATION

On the journey of nurturing a child with special needs, communication becomes a symphony of connection. It is an interplay of understanding, empathy, self-expression, and self-advocacy. As we tune our hearts to our child's unique frequency, we unlock doors to their thoughts, emotions, and aspirations.

Effective communication with children of diverse needs is an ongoing journey that unfolds with patience, understanding, and a commitment to connecting with our children on their terms. By embracing a variety of communication techniques and fostering active listening and empathy, we nurture an environment where every child can thrive, communicate, and flourish.

Through this shared dialogue, we unlock the incredible potential within each child and cultivate bonds that transcend words. The ability to self-express and self-advocate empowers them to navigate a world that may not always understand their unique needs. As caregivers, we are entrusted with the privilege of helping our children find their voices, assert their rights, and ultimately flourish as confident individuals.

In this journey of empowerment, we create a harmonious melody—a beautiful testament to the power of understanding, empathy, and self-expression. It is a celebration of our children's unique abilities, their voices, and the bonds that connect us heart to heart.

REFLECTIONS

How do you celebrate and embrace the uniqueness of your child's communication style?

_____

_____

_____

_____

_____

In what ways have you empowered your child to self-advocate and express his/her needs, fostering his/her self-confidence and independence?

_____

_____

_____

_____

_____

How do you actively listen to your child, not just with your ears, but with your heart, understanding his/her emotions and thoughts, as well as his/her words?

_____

_____

_____

_____

_____

What creative outlets have you provided for your child to celebrate self-expression through art, music, or play?

_____

_____

_____

_____

_____

How have you stepped into your child's shoes to see the world through his/her eyes, deepening your connection and fostering trust and open communication?

_____

_____

_____

_____

_____

AFFIRMATIONS

1. I celebrate and cherish my child's unique means of communication.
2. I empower my child to express their needs and assert their preferences with confidence.
3. I am a compassionate and active listener, nurturing deep connections with my child.

THOUGHTS TO PONDER

"The purposes of a person's heart are deep waters, but one who has insight draws them out." (Proverbs 20:5 – NIV).

"Empathy is about finding echoes of another person in yourself."
—Mohsin Hamid

NOTE TO SELF

_____

_____

_____

_____

_____

SELF-CARE CORNER - A DIALOGUE

This is a heartfelt conversation between a mother (Sarah) and son (Alex).

Sarah: Good morning, sweetie. How did you sleep last night?

Alex: Morning, Mom. I slept okay. I had a dream about flying. It was fun.

Sarah: That sounds amazing, Alex. I'd love to hear more about your dream. *(She smiles warmly).*

Alex: *(with enthusiasm)* I was soaring above the fields, just like the birds we saw last weekend. It was like I could touch the clouds, Mom.

Sarah: *(gratefully)* Wow, that must have been a fantastic dream. It's fascinating to hear about it. *(She sits beside him).*

Alex: Mom, do you remember that story you read me last night? About the adventures of the little bear?

Sarah: *(nodding)* Yes, I do. Did you enjoy the story?

Alex: *(enthusiastically)* I loved it, Mom! The bear was so brave. I wish I could be like him sometimes.

Sarah: You are very brave, Alex. You face every day with such courage, just like that little bear. *(She squeezes his hand gently).*

Alex: *(thoughtfully)* You think so, Mom? Sometimes, I find it hard to talk to the other kids at school.

Sarah: *(encouragingly)* It's okay, Sweetie. I understand that it can be challenging, but you know, there are many ways to communicate. We'll keep working on it together.

Alex: Thanks, Mom. You're the best. *(He gives her a big smile).*

Sarah: *(gratefully)* You're the best too, Alex. We make a great team. Remember, no matter what, I'm here to listen, understand, and help you with anything you need.

Alex: *(with a glimmer in his eye)* I know, Mom. And I'm lucky to have you.

Sarah: *(teary-eyed)* I'm even luckier to have you, my incredible, dream-soaring son. *(She gives him a loving hug).*

CHAPTER 5

UNLOCKING YOUR CHILD'S SKILLS

Within every child, there exists a unique constellation of abilities, an array of talents waiting to be discovered and nurtured. As parents and caregivers of children with special needs, our privilege and responsibility are to unlock their potential. We must provide the fertile ground for their skills to flourish, their passions to thrive, and their individuality to shine.

IDENTIFYING AND NURTURING STRENGTHS AND INTERESTS

The process of identifying a child's strengths and interests is akin to uncovering hidden gems in a treasure chest. It demands keen observation, patience, and an open heart. Children with special needs, like all children, possess innate strengths—whether in academics, arts, sports, or creative endeavors. Nurturing these strengths is a testament to their individuality and a key to fostering a sense of accomplishment and self-worth. In a world where differences are sometimes met with ridicule, nurturing strengths becomes a cornerstone of building confidence, resilience, and a strong sense of self.

Observation and Exploration - Close observation is the lens through which we gain insights into our child's interactions, preferences, and reactions. What activities bring them joy? What subjects or tasks capture their attention? Through careful exploration and experimentation, we unveil the landscapes of their interests. Childhood exploration is a vital part of this journey. It is through exploration that children find areas of interest, as well as discover their own capabilities.

As caregivers, our role is to provide a safe and supportive environment that allows children to explore and uncover their interests. Sometimes, this might mean giving them space to play and experiment, even if it leads to some mess or chaos. These exploratory moments help children discover where their true passions lie.

Encouragement and Reinforcement - Encouragement serves as the nurturing soil in which talents take root and flourish. When our children make efforts, no matter how small, it is crucial to acknowledge and celebrate those achievements. Whether it is a drawing, a new word, or a small milestone, these accomplishments deserve recognition. No matter the outcome, praising their efforts communicates our support and belief in their potential.

In addition to praise, it is essential to provide opportunities for children to delve deeper into areas that pique their curiosity. Depending on their abilities and interests, this may involve enrolling them in classes, seeking out mentors, or simply dedicating time to explore together as a family. By actively participating in their pursuits, we reinforce our support and create opportunities for bonding and shared growth.

It is important to note that, as caregivers, we may have concerns or reservations about certain activities or interests due to our child's unique needs. While some activities may be off-limits for safety or health reasons, we should seek alternatives or adapt activities to ensure their participation wherever possible. The journey to unlock our child's skills is a collaborative one, and we play a pivotal role in nurturing their talents and fostering their individuality.

Our commitment to identifying and nurturing our child's strengths and interests reflects our belief in their limitless potential. It is a testament to our love, support, and dedication to helping them flourish in their own unique way.

TAILORING EDUCATION AND LEARNING STRATEGIES TO YOUR CHILD'S NEEDS

Education is not a one-size-fits-all endeavor; it is one filled with a diversity of learning styles, strengths, and challenges. Tailoring educational strategies to your child's needs is a journey of customization that honors their unique path and equips them with the tools they need to succeed. As parents and caregivers, it is our responsibility to remain open to learning, to collaborate with educators and therapists, and to seek the knowledge and resources necessary to help our children with special needs thrive.

Differentiated Instruction - In special needs education, differentiated instruction takes center stage. This approach involves customizing teaching methods, materials, and assessments to match each child's learning styles and abilities. It ensures that education is not only accessible but also engaging, aligning seamlessly with your child's strengths.

When educators embrace differentiated instruction, they create an inclusive learning environment where every child's unique abilities are celebrated. By recognizing and accommodating diverse learning styles, children with special needs can engage with the curriculum at their own pace and in their preferred way. This tailored approach ensures that no child is left behind and that each one has the opportunity to reach their full potential.

Incorporating Sensory-Friendly Learning - For children with sensory sensitivities, the learning environment plays a pivotal role in their educational journey. Sensory-friendly strategies are designed to create a space where sensory challenges are minimized, allowing your child to focus, process information, and engage with educational activities more effectively. By providing a calm and sensory-responsive setting, educators and caregivers offer support that can significantly enhance your child's learning experience.

Sensory-friendly learning environments may include adjustments like reducing sensory distractions, providing sensory tools, and creating designated quiet spaces. These modifications empower children to engage with the learning process while managing sensory sensitivities effectively.

COLLABORATION FOR HOLISTIC DEVELOPMENT

The journey of nurturing your child's potential is not a solitary one—it is a collaborative endeavor that bridges home, school, and therapy settings. Collaborating with educators and therapists fosters a holistic approach to development, ensuring that your child's growth is nurtured comprehensively.

Open Communication - Establishing open lines of communication with educators and therapists is paramount. Sharing insights about your child's strengths, needs, and preferences empowers them to create a tailored and supportive learning environment. As a parent or caregiver, you serve as your child's advocate, and effective communication with their educational team is essential to ensure they receive the support they need.

Goal Setting and Progress Tracking - Collaborative goal setting is vital to your child's educational journey. Working with educators and therapists to establish realistic and achievable goals creates a roadmap for your child's development. These goals provide a framework for monitoring progress and making necessary adjustments along the way. It ensures that your child's educational plan remains dynamic, adapting to their evolving needs and abilities.

UNLOCKING A BRIGHT FUTURE: A COLLABORATIVE LEGACY

As we invest our time, energy, and love into unlocking our child's skills and potential, we are crafting a legacy that extends far beyond the present moment. By nurturing their strengths, tailoring education to their needs, and collaborating with educators and therapists, we are planting seeds of possibility that will continue to flourish throughout their lives.

Together, we will unveil the extraordinary wonder of abilities that lies within your child, illuminating a path towards a future brimming with promise and endless potential. The collaborative legacy you create today will be a guiding light for your child's journey, inspiring them to embrace their uniqueness and pursue their dreams with confidence and determination.

REFLECTIONS

How can you actively engage in the process of tailoring education to meet your child's unique needs and learning style?

_____

_____

_____

_____

_____

What specific strategies have you employed to create a sensory-friendly learning environment for your child with special needs?

_____

_____

_____

_____

In what ways have you effectively communicated with your child's educators and therapists to ensure a collaborative and holistic approach to their development?

_____

_____

_____

_____

_____

How can you set realistic and achievable goals in collaboration with educators and therapists to track your child's progress effectively?

_____

_____

_____

_____

_____

What steps can you take to nurture your child's skills, celebrate their strengths, and equip them for a future filled with promise and endless potential?

_____

_____

_____

_____

_____

AFFIRMATIONS

1. I am committed to tailoring education to my child's unique needs, unlocking their full potential.
2. I create a sensory-friendly learning environment that empowers my child to engage effectively with the curriculum.
3. I am a dedicated advocate for my child, fostering open communication and collaboration for their holistic development.

THOUGHTS TO PONDER

"Start children off on the way they should go, and even when they are old they will not turn from it." (Proverbs 22:6 – NIV).

"Education is not the filling of a pail, but the lighting of a fire."
—*William Butler Yeats*

NOTE TO SELF

_____

_____

_____

_____

_____

SELF-CARE CORNER

Abba Father,

As I navigate this journey with my precious child, I bow my head in gratitude for the unique constellation of abilities they possess. You have entrusted me with the privilege and responsibility of nurturing their potential, and for that, I am deeply thankful.

I pray for the wisdom to identify and nurture their strengths and interests and to recognize the hidden gems within their heart. May I always observe, explore, and encourage them with patience and love.

Guide me in tailoring their education to their distinctive needs, embracing differentiated instruction, and creating a sensory-friendly learning environment. Let me be their advocate in collaboration with educators and therapists, fostering open communication, setting meaningful goals, and tracking their progress.

Together, may we unlock the boundless possibilities within my child, planting seeds of promise that will continue to bloom throughout their life. May this journey be a testament to the love, dedication, and belief in their limitless potential.

Amen.

CHAPTER 6

ADVOCATING FOR SUPPORTIVE LEARNING ENVIRONMENTS

Education is the beacon that lights the path to empowerment, where dreams and potential take root and flourish. Inclusive education amplifies this beacon, ensuring that it shines on every child, regardless of their abilities. It is a commitment to providing an environment where every child can learn, grow, and thrive, and it is a duty we, as parents and caregivers, passionately uphold.

On our journey to champion inclusive education, we are essentially dismantling barriers that stand in the way of our children's progress. We become advocates, working tirelessly to break down the walls of exclusion and create learning environments that nurture every child. It is a path fraught with challenges, but we embark on it with determination and a sense of purpose.

One fundamental truth we must embrace is that not all teachers are experts in special needs education. However, as parents and caregivers, we are experts when it comes to our children. This realization carries with it the responsibility of continuous learning. We immerse ourselves in the world of special needs education, empowering us to make informed decisions and initiate conversations that will benefit our children. In doing so, we navigate the complex landscape of education, ensuring our children's needs are met.

It is vital to acknowledge that the path to inclusive education is not always straightforward. Not every teacher or school environment readily adapts to the unique requirements of our children. Some may be hesitant to change established practices, and this is where our role as advocates becomes crucial. We advocate for our children and all children who need an inclusive education. We engage in open, respectful, and proactive dialogues with educators and institutions, sparking change and creating learning environments where every child can thrive.

While it is our fervent hope to find schools and educators who are open to the principles of inclusive education, we must also be prepared for the occasional hiccups along the way. There are no perfect institutions, and challenges may arise from time to time. In such moments, we remain composed, seeking solutions that best serve our children's needs. We remember that our role is to ensure that the learning environment aligns with our children's growth and development.

As we navigate the journey of inclusive education, we do so with the understanding that it is a shared responsibility. Together with educators, therapists, and other caregivers, we shape a world where every child is valued, nurtured, and empowered to reach their full potential.

ADVOCATING FOR INCLUSIVE EDUCATION

Inclusive education is not merely a concept; it stands as a fundamental right, a belief that every child deserves access to quality education regardless of their abilities. In many countries, the Ministry or Department of Education often echoes this belief in their mottos or slogans, such as "Every Child Can Learn, Every Child Must Learn" in Jamaica, and the "No Child Left Behind Act of 2001" in the United States of America. Depending on your country of residence, a quick online search with your country's education department can provide you with invaluable insights into the policies and principles that guide inclusive education.

Advocating for inclusive education involves shedding light on the unique challenges that children with special needs face, and advocating for solutions that break down barriers, creating an educational environment where every child can thrive.

Rights and Legislation - Understanding the legal framework that surrounds inclusive education equips parents and caregivers with the knowledge they need to assert their child's right to education. Legislation such as the Individuals with Disabilities Education Act (IDEA) in the United States and the Equality Act 2010 in the United Kingdom mandates that children with disabilities are entitled to a free and appropriate public education in the least restrictive environment. While the legal landscape may vary in developing countries, exploring available resources through special education units or related governmental bodies is still crucial.

Many countries worldwide have ratified the United Nations Convention on the Rights of Persons with Disabilities (UNCRPD), further solidifying the provisions for children with special needs. It is incumbent upon parents and caregivers to unearth this information and use it as a powerful tool in advocating for their children. Amid the complexities and challenges of advocacy, keeping our "why" at the forefront is vital. Advocating for children with special needs is no small feat, and it can sometimes become overwhelming. However, our commitment to their growth and development as responsible global citizens fuels our determination to navigate this path.

Challenges and Solutions - Inclusive education, like any meaningful endeavor, is not without its challenges. From attitudinal barriers to the scarcity of resources, the road to inclusion can indeed be bumpy. Each challenge, however, presents an opportunity for change and transformation. Collaborating with schools, engaging in open dialogues with educators, and advocating for necessary accommodations and support services can pave the way for innovative solutions that convert challenges into stepping stones toward a more inclusive future.

It is important for parents and caregivers not to internalize everything they encounter on this journey. Often, the attitudes of others towards special needs or neurodiversity are reflective of the individuals themselves and not a judgment of you or your children. Embracing this perspective empowers you to continue advocating for the rights and needs of your children, ensuring they have every opportunity to receive the education they deserve.

COLLABORATION BETWEEN PARENTS, TEACHERS, AND SPECIALISTS

In inclusive education, the cornerstone upon which this harmonious relationship is built is collaboration. It is a delicate dance where parents, teachers, specialists, and advocates come together, working in harmony to create a cohesive and enriching learning environment. While it is true that not everyone may be readily open to collaboration, be it due to fear, reluctance, or even the potential dissolution of the blame game, it is crucial to remain focused and steadfast in your efforts to collaborate with teachers and specialists for the betterment of your children.

Open Communication - Effective communication, a mainstay of collaboration, forms the bedrock upon which inclusive education thrives. Regular meetings, updates on progress, and open dialogues create an environment where insights and strategies can be openly shared. This ensures that the child's needs are addressed comprehensively and with a holistic approach in mind.

By keeping the channels of communication open and flowing, a bridge is built connecting the wisdom of parents, the expertise of teachers, and the insights of specialists. This collaboration results in a more complete understanding of the child's unique requirements, fostering a learning environment that caters to their needs. While it is true that not all collaborations will be without friction, each interaction and conversation contributes to the ongoing development of strategies and solutions to better serve the child.

Shared Goals and Individual Plans - Collaboration thrives when all parties involved share a common goal: the well-being and success of the child. Through this shared vision, collaboration becomes not just a responsibility but a deeply rewarding endeavor. One of the essential tools for achieving this synergy is the creation of individualized education plans (IEPs).

IEPs, while not a universal feature in every institution, serve as a roadmap for a child's educational journey. When parents, teachers, and specialists collaborate to develop these plans, it ensures that the child's unique strengths and challenges are comprehensively addressed. By tailoring education to match a child's needs and abilities, IEPs are a testament to the power of collaboration in action.

As parents and caregivers, our aim is to work alongside teachers and specialists to help our children achieve their educational and developmental milestones as effectively as possible. Whether you encounter structured IEPs or not, the spirit of collaboration remains at the core of the process. Each child is unique, and the most holistic and effective educational strategies can be developed through the combined insights, efforts, and expertise of all involved parties.

CRAFTING INCLUSIVE CLASSROOMS AND DIVERSE TEACHING METHODS

We must recognize that true inclusion surpasses mere physical presence in the classroom. It necessitates the adaptation of both classroom environments and teaching methods to address the diverse needs of every child. As parents and caregivers, we may not be the ones implementing these teaching methods, but our advocacy for accommodations and modifications is paramount. It is important to remember that accommodations do not offer our children an unfair advantage; instead, they seek to diminish their disadvantages, leveling the playing field for all, thereby, providing equity.

Universal Design for Learning (UDL) - A pivotal framework in inclusive education is Universal Design for Learning (UDL).

This framework tailors education to accommodate diverse learning styles and abilities. By providing multiple avenues for students to engage with content, express their comprehension, and showcase their skills, UDL ensures that every child can access and reap the benefits of the curriculum.

Accommodations and Modifications - In the inclusive classroom, accommodations and modifications are key tools. Accommodations are designed to make adjustments to the learning environment or process, ensuring that it is accessible to all students. On the other hand, modifications involve altering the curriculum itself. These strategies are fundamental in guaranteeing that each child can participate and achieve success at their unique pace.

BUILDING A LEGACY OF INCLUSION

The essence of inclusive education encapsulates a legacy of inclusion, empathy, and the belief in every child's boundless potential. Our journey involves advocating for rights, collaborating to overcome challenges, and adapting our approaches to create a foundation that transforms education into an open gateway of opportunity for all.

As parents and caregivers, our task is to support the holistic development of our children, nurturing their strengths and addressing their challenges. This journey, underpinned by the principles of inclusive education, lays the groundwork for each child to thrive and embrace their future as responsible global citizens.

REFLECTION

How can you become more informed about the rights and legislations that protect your child's access to inclusive education, and what steps can you take to advocate for these rights?

_____

_____

_____

_____

_____

How can you contribute to creating a more inclusive classroom environment for your child?

_____

_____

_____

_____

In what ways have accommodations and modifications proven beneficial in your child's learning journey?

_____

_____

_____

_____

How can you further advocate for your child's right to an inclusive education in your local community?

_____

_____

_____

_____

_____

AFFIRMATIONS

1. I am committed to understanding and advocating for the rights and legislations that ensure my child's access to quality, inclusive education.
2. I am a strong advocate for inclusive education and actively work to create supportive learning environments for my child.
3. I believe that accommodations and modifications are essential tools that empower my child to succeed.

THOUGHTS TO PONDER

"Let us not become weary in doing good, for at the proper time we will reap a harvest if we do not give up." (Galatians 6:9 – NIV).

"Inclusion is not a matter of political correctness. It is the key to growth." —Jesse Jackson

NOTE TO SELF

_____

_____

_____

_____

_____

SELF-CARE CORNER - A POEM

Inclusion's melody, a song so bright,
Where all children's stars shine through the night.
With advocates, we stand hand in hand,
Crafting a future, strong and grand.

In classrooms diverse, we find the key,
Unlocking potential, setting spirits free.
In every child, we see dreams take flight.
Inclusion's symphony, a beacon of light.

CHAPTER 7

PRACTICAL STRATEGIES FOR DAILY LIFE

L ife requires the development of various skills to create independence, self-expression, and meaningful connections. For children with special needs, skillset development is a journey of empowerment—one that equips them with the tools to navigate daily life, manage challenges, and forge lasting relationships. As guides on this voyage, we must nurture a holistic skillset that prepares them for today and a future of possibilities. As much as possible, we should aim to have our children become gradually independent as they mature. I am a firm believer that we should aim to parent well, so as our children grow, they will become less dependent on us as parents and more independent. It really isn't a nice reality for our children to grow, and their maturity and independence do not grow as well. Now, when nurturing our special needs children, this will be some of our realities. In this regard, we will need to exercise wisdom by planning ahead for respite care and the legalities should we pass before our children.

PROMOTING INDEPENDENCE AND LIFE SKILLS DEVELOPMENT

Independence is the North Star that guides our children towards self-sufficiency, confidence, and a sense of achievement.

Fostering life skills is a testament to their capabilities, enabling them to confidently navigate the world. Depending on our young one's age and capabilities, we can start skill development by involving them in daily chores. I know this is no easy feat for most, but we should endeavor to have them involved nonetheless.

Task Analysis: Breaking down tasks into manageable steps empowers children to approach challenges systematically. We instill a sense of competence and mastery by providing clear instructions and visual support. Clear instructions and visual support help our children tremendously. Alarms and timers can be useful for those affected by time blindness. We will have to teach our young ones how to use these to their advantage.

Daily Routines: Routines offer a scaffold upon which independence is built. Establishing consistent routines for tasks like dressing, mealtime, and hygiene fosters a sense of predictability and control. Depending on our young one's diagnosis, routines can be a real challenge, and sometimes they relapse. I encourage you to keep at it; do not give up, and take it one step at a time. Sometimes, we may need to take a step or two back to where our children are and work with them to get them forward.

STRATEGIES FOR MANAGING BEHAVIORS AND CHALLENGES

Managing behaviours and challenges is vital to skillset development. Understanding triggers, cultivating coping strategies, and fostering self-regulation empower children to navigate emotional landscapes with resilience. It is important that we help our children identify and understand their triggers and teach them coping strategies. Teaching our children about the illness they have been diagnosed with and helping them to identify areas of strength to build on and areas of weakness to navigate makes a huge difference. The fact is, whether or not we tell them of their diagnosis, they know they have different issues compared to their peers. While we do not encourage comparisons, they are aware that their realities vary from their peers.

Behavioral Support Plans: Crafting behavioral support plans that identify triggers, interventions, and positive reinforcement strategies helps manage challenging behaviors. Consistency and collaboration ensure a unified approach across various settings. In this regard, we may need to enlist the help of trained professionals, such as a therapist or a coach, if applicable.

Managing behaviour is not a one size fits all endeavor. Some techniques and strategies will work for some children and not work for others. If what we have been trying is not working, we must try other approaches. Likewise, the same behavioral interventions may not be applicable to every diagnosis. I have mentioned before that this is no easy feat; believe me, for those parents and caregivers who have to manage behaviour, please know it is not easy from personal experience. But I can tell you, you can do hard things. Maintaining a calm and composed demeanor with our young ones is important:

1. So that we remain in control of the situation as the adult, and
2. We are modeling the appropriate behaviours they can emulate.

As a parent or caregiver, if you cannot enlist a trainer professional's assistance, you can create a behaviour support plan for your children. Now, the key thing here is making the decision to do so. It can't be done half-heartedly, as some days will be very difficult compared to others. After taking the decision, reflect on your children's behaviour. What are the usual triggers? What are possible interventions that can be used? This is a behavioral intervention plan in its simplest form, and it is quite manageable for parents and caregivers. Technically, it involves more, however, parents and caregivers can use this simplified approach and experience improvement.

Coping and Regulation Techniques: Equipping children with coping techniques—such as deep breathing, sensory breaks, and mindfulness exercises—enables them to navigate moments of stress and anxiety. By fostering emotional self-regulation, we empower them to face challenges head-on.

1. According to DiLonardo (2023), deep breathing is also known as belly breathing and can be quite refreshing. Here are ten steps to getting it right:

   - Find a comfy, quiet spot where you won't be bothered. You can sit or lie down, but if you're sitting, sit up straight and keep your feet flat on the floor. Close your eyes.
   - Place one hand on your belly, right under your ribs, and put the other hand on your chest.
   - Take a normal breath.
   - Now, take a slow, deep breath. Breathe in slowly through your nose. Notice how your belly rises under your hand.

- Hold your breath for a second or two.
- Breathe out slowly through your mouth. Watch your hand on your belly go in as you breathe out.
- Keep doing this a few times until you find a calming rhythm.
- Now, add some imagination to your breathing. When you breathe in, picture that the air is bringing relaxation and calmness to your whole body.
- As you breathe out, imagine that your breath is carrying away stress and tension.
- Try to deep breathe for ten minutes or until you start feeling more relaxed and less stressed. You can gradually aim for 15-20 minutes over time. It is your special time to unwind and feel better.

2. A sensory break is a preset time that allows a student to deescalate from the sensory stimulation of the classroom setting. The student is allowed to go outside the classroom and use the trampoline, ball pit or gym. Some schools, in particular, do not have these resources. What can be done then is to allow the students to take a walk outside and inhale some fresh air. It is important to note that sensory breaks are not earned; they should be a part of the children's daily routine once they are required.

3. Mindfulness can be very simply described as living in the moment. In essence, it is paying attention to what is happening now, in each moment. Mindfulness has the ability to reduce stress and increase awareness. Activities that promote mindfulness are those that allow the

student's mind to slow and focus on the task at hand. For example, this may be achieved through coloring and taking pictures of nature. Deep breathing can also be incorporated into mindfulness and practiced as meditation.

ENHANCING SOCIAL INTERACTIONS AND RELATIONSHIPS

We are social beings, hence the importance of social interactions and relationships. Social interactions can then be seen as the fabric of human connection that enriches lives, fosters friendships, and nurtures a sense of belonging. Enhancing social skills opens doors to meaningful relationships and a vibrant social life. Everyone has an innate need for a sense of belonging. We come from families that are part of communities, that are a part of districts, parishes/states, and ultimately, countries, regions and the world. Subsequently, we must belong somewhere.

Some of our beautiful young souls with special needs are able to maintain social interactions and relationships, while others will struggle. Those diagnosed as being on the Autism Spectrum, for example, or even Autistic traits, will struggle with social cues and maintaining relationships. Some diagnosed with ADHD may also find themselves with challenges in this area. Let me hasten to say these are not the only ones with social challenges. It then becomes our duty as parents and caregivers to help them navigate this space.

Social Stories and Role-Playing: Social stories and role-playing provide a safe space to practice social interactions and etiquette. Children build confidence and competence in social settings by rehearsing scenarios and behaviors. You may brainstorm some common social interactions and share stories about these, such as what a class party may be like versus a class trip or even a school barbeque. After sharing these stories, the scenario can then be role-played. Be creative and switch roles with your children; help them to imagine what it would be like and help them identify feelings and emotions and, where applicable, articulate such. Be mindful that some of our children will need help articulating their feelings; pictures can be used to help them identify their feelings.

Peer Interactions and Playgroups: Facilitating interactions with peers, whether through playgroups or collaborative activities, creates opportunities for social growth. Structured playdates encourage shared experiences and the development of social bonds. I know some of us are hesitant to take our children out. However, it is important that our children interact with society. Do not hide them away for fear of discrimination; take them out. Unfortunately, discrimination is an experience we will face as parents and caregivers of special needs children. What we can do is educate those who genuinely care and don't take any of it personally.

CRAFTING A HOLISTIC LEGACY BY NURTURING SKILLSET MASTERY

As we nurture a holistic skillset, we are sowing seeds of empowerment that will blossom throughout a child's life. By promoting independence, managing behaviors, and enhancing social interactions, we create a legacy of resilience, self-expression, and meaningful relationships, thereby empowering our children to become responsible global citizens.

REFLECTION

How can you balance fostering independence with providing necessary support for your child's unique needs?

_____

_____

_____

_____

_____

What steps can you take to ensure that your children continue to grow in maturity and independence as they navigate life with special needs?

_____

_____

_____

_____

_____

How can you best prepare for unforeseen circumstances and plan for the long-term care of your child?

_____

_____

_____

_____

_____

In what ways can you help your child become a responsible global citizen as they mature and grow more independent?

_____

_____

_____

_____

_____

AFFIRMATIONS

1. I believe in my child's potential for growth, independence, and resilience.
2. I am committed to nurturing a holistic skillset that equips my child for a future filled with possibilities.
3. I celebrate every step my child takes toward greater independence and self-sufficiency.

THOUGHTS TO PONDER

"Train up a child in the way he should go: and when he is old, he will not depart from it." (Proverbs 22:6 – KJV).

"The way to develop the best that is in a person is by appreciation and encouragement." —Charles Schwab

NOTE TO SELF

_____

_____

_____

SELF-CARE CORNER - A LETTER TO SELF

Dear Self,

As we journey through your life, I wanted to take a moment to remind you of the vital role you play in nurturing our child's holistic skillset. You are weaving a legacy of empowerment, resilience, and self-expression every day.

Your commitment to promoting independence is unwavering. By involving our child in daily chores and breaking down tasks into manageable steps, you provide the tools they need to navigate life with confidence. Clear instructions and visual supports are your allies in this journey, empowering them to approach challenges systematically.

Despite the occasional relapse, establishing consistent routines creates a sense of predictability and control. Remember, taking steps back is sometimes necessary to move forward, and you have shown remarkable patience and determination in doing so.

When managing behaviors and challenges, you have been our child's anchor. Understanding triggers, crafting behavioral support plans, and fostering self-regulation are your tools for nurturing their emotional landscapes with resilience. It is a journey that is no doubt challenging, but your calm and composed demeanor sets the example and paves the way.

When it comes to enhancing social interactions and relationships, your dedication shines through. You have created safe spaces for practicing social interactions, such as social stories and role-playing, and facilitated peer interactions through playgroups. Remember that taking our child out into the world is essential despite the challenges.

As you continue to nurture this holistic legacy, you are sowing seeds of empowerment that will bloom throughout our child's life. You are empowering them to become responsible global citizens, and for that, you should be immensely proud of yourself.

With admiration and gratitude,
Vanesia

CHAPTER 8

RECOGNIZING MILESTONES AND ACHIEVEMENTS

As each child develops, every progress, no matter how small, is a stroke of brilliance—an affirmation of resilience, determination, and the boundless capacity for growth. Our role as caregivers of children with special needs involves acknowledging the grand achievements and celebrating the subtle victories that illuminate their unique path. By setting goals, fostering a culture of appreciation, and honoring their individual journey, we lay the groundwork for a future teeming with possibilities.

Setting Realistic Goals and Celebrating Small Victories - Goals serve as the compass guiding our efforts, the map charting the course of progress. The foundation for celebrating achievements rests upon the establishment of realistic goals that align with a child's abilities. Every step forward, no matter how incremental, is indeed a victory worthy of celebration.

For instance, consider the SMART goal of a child being able to work independently. By making this goal Specific, Measurable, Achievable, Relevant, and Time-bound, we create a clear pathway for progress. This might involve specifying that the child will complete a particular task independently, measuring their success by tracking the number of times they achieve it, ensuring it is attainable for their skill level, relevant to their growth, and setting a realistic timeframe for achieving it.

Small Steps, Big Impact - Small victories constitute the building blocks of monumental accomplishments. Celebrating each milestone, no matter how modest it may appear, significantly reinforces a sense of accomplishment. Moreover, it acts as a source of motivation, encouraging children to persist and continue on their unique journey of development.

In our example, if the child's goal is to work independently, small victories could be celebrated each time they successfully complete a part of the task autonomously. These smaller achievements help build their confidence and determination, motivating them to tackle the larger goal of full independence.

Each small success not only signifies progress but also symbolizes a step closer to realizing their full potential. It empowers the child and reassures them that they can overcome obstacles and achieve their goals with determination and the right support system. It is about acknowledging that every step forward, no matter how small, is indeed a victory worth celebrating. It is an acknowledgment that growth and progress are achieved one step at a time.

CREATING A CULTURE OF APPRECIATION AND GROWTH

Celebration is not merely an event; it is a culture that should be deeply ingrained in nurturing children with special needs. This culture is one of appreciation, encouragement, and recognition. It fosters an environment where children feel seen, heard, and empowered. The journey of raising children with special needs is challenging and filled with unique triumphs and obstacles.

Celebrating achievements, both small and large, plays a vital role in providing children with the encouragement they need to thrive. It bolsters their self-esteem and motivation, making them aware of their progress and potential. It also helps the parents and caregivers, acknowledging the fruit of their labour and sometimes gives the feeling of satisfaction needed.

Praise and Positive Reinforcement - Positive reinforcement is about encouraging a pattern of desired behavior by offering a reward. Wisdom is essential in guiding this process, ensuring a balance.

Praise and positive reinforcement often have a ripple effect. When a child is consistently acknowledged for their accomplishments, they are more likely to be motivated to keep trying and pushing their boundaries. It becomes a cycle of growth and success as the child's self-esteem and belief in their abilities continue to rise.

Creating Rituals of Celebration - Establishing rituals of celebration adds structure and anticipation to a child's life. Whether it is a weekly progress check-in, a special treat, or a family celebration, these rituals create anchors of positivity in a child's world. They feel motivated and valued when they know that there are special moments dedicated to recognizing their achievements.

A weekly progress check-in, for example, can be an excellent way to acknowledge small steps forward and provide an opportunity to discuss goals and aspirations. A special treat, whether a favorite meal or activity, can be a tangible reward for effort and achievement. Family celebrations bring everyone together to commemorate the child's accomplishments, fostering a sense of unity and appreciation within the family.

HONORING YOUR CHILD'S UNIQUE PATH AND ACCOMPLISHMENTS

Every child's journey is a masterpiece, a unique canvas painted with their own hues of strengths, challenges, and triumphs. Each one treads a path that is distinctly their own, with its own set of obstacles and victories. Honoring their individual path and accomplishments is an ode to their uniqueness—a testament to their worth and potential.

Celebrating Effort and Persistence - Celebration is not limited to outcomes; it encompasses the effort, determination, and courage displayed throughout the journey. By acknowledging the effort, we validate the tenacity and perseverance that drive progress. Effort is often an unspoken hero, as many children with special needs exert considerable effort to accomplish what others might find simple. It is crucial to recognize this effort and acknowledge the strength it demonstrates.

Championing Individuality - The beauty of celebrating progress lies in its individuality. What may seem small to one child may be monumental to another. We create an inclusive and affirming environment by championing each child's unique path. It is a reminder that there is no universal yardstick for progress. What matters most is the journey that the child undertakes and the challenges they overcome. Championing individuality sends the message that their path is honored and their accomplishments celebrated, regardless of how they compare to others.

A LEGACY OF CELEBRATION NURTURING GROWTH AND RESILIENCE

By celebrating progress, we are nurturing a legacy of growth, resilience, and belief in the potential of every child. The culture of appreciation and growth we foster provides a strong foundation for their future. It reinforces the understanding that, regardless of their unique challenges, they can overcome obstacles and achieve greatness. In celebrating their achievements and the journey that leads to them, we remind children that their individuality is cherished and their potential is limitless.

REFLECTION

How can you integrate a culture of celebration and appreciation into your child's daily life to motivate their progress and self-esteem?

_____

_____

_____

_____

_____

What are some specific rituals of celebration that you can establish within your family to honor your child's unique achievements?

_____

_____

_____

_____

In what ways can you ensure that you champion your child's individuality and progress, regardless of how it compares to others?

_____

_____

_____

_____

_____

How has celebrating small victories positively impacted your child's journey, and what strategies can you further develop to celebrate their resilience and growth?

_____

_____

_____

_____

_____

AFFIRMATIONS

1. I celebrate every step of my child's unique journey, knowing that each small victory is a testament to their resilience and potential.
2. Praise and positive reinforcement are powerful tools to boost my child's self-esteem and motivation, and I use them to consistently acknowledge their efforts and achievements.
3. By championing my child's individuality and honoring their accomplishments, I create a supportive and affirming environment that fosters their growth and self-worth.

THOUGHTS TO PONDER

"For we are God's handiwork, created in Christ Jesus to do good works, which God prepared in advance for us to do." (Ephesians 2:10 - NIV).

"Success is not final, failure is not fatal: It is the courage to continue that counts." —Winston Churchill

NOTE TO SELF

_____

_____

_____

_____

_____

SELF-CARE CORNER - A JINGLE

In the symphony of your journey, each note you play,
A melody of progress, in your unique way.
With every step forward, no matter how small,
You dance towards greatness, giving your all.

Setting goals like a compass, guiding your quest,
In your world of achievements, you're truly the best.
Small steps, big impacts, building a dream,
Each victory celebrated, a star in your gleam.

A culture of appreciation, a quilt of care,
In praise and reinforcement, love fills the air.
Rituals of celebration, moments so grand,
In your world of achievements, you take a stand.

Honor your path, so unique and so bright,
Effort and persistence, your guiding light.
Champion your individuality, let your heart soar,

In your legacy of celebration, you'll achieve even more.

A legacy of growth, resilience, and grace,
In your journey's embrace, you find your place.
With unwavering belief in your potential's embrace,
Celebrate your progress, you're winning life's race.

CHAPTER 9

NAVIGATING LEGAL AND FINANCIAL ASPECTS

In the realm of nurturing children with special needs, the journey is not only one of emotional growth but also of navigating the intricate landscapes of legal rights, financial considerations, and accessing the resources that pave the way for a brighter future. As caregivers, parents, and advocates, it is essential to be well-informed about the legal and financial aspects that impact the well-being and development of our children. It is easy to stay in your little corner, doing your own little thing; however, seeking resources, services, and support is paramount. The saying is true: closed mouths don't get fed. Make phone calls and ask those in a position to give support or direct you to where you can access this support. As a general thought, a good place to start is with the Ministry or Department of Education— special education to be specific—the Ministry or Department of Health, Child Development or Mental Health as is relevant and the agency or department that deals with national insurance.

ACCESSING RESOURCES, SERVICES, AND FINANCIAL SUPPORT

Navigating the complex web of resources and services available to children with special needs can be daunting, yet it is a journey of empowerment—a quest to secure the tools and support necessary for their growth and development. When we approach those places named above, we will then be directed to the other relevant authorities as may be the case. Remember, every child is unique; hence, their needs will vary. Do not become overwhelmed by having to visit different offices. Stay focused on the goal, which is access to resources and services as well as financial support as may be needed. Children with special needs usually have more intricate needs; for example, in many cases, a special need or disability does not exist in isolation, the child may have another health condition, special dietary considerations, and so on.

When you finally get into these offices to access support in whichever form, please have a clear mind, take a notepad and pen, make your jottings, and ask relevant questions. Your goal here is to leave with a thorough understanding so you can make informed decisions to benefit your children.

Resource Navigation: Understanding the array of services and supports—from educational programs to therapy services to community organizations—empowers you to make informed decisions that cater to your child's unique needs.

Financial Assistance: Exploring financial support options, such as government programs, grants, and medical insurance, ensures that financial constraints do not hinder your child's access to essential services.

LEGAL RIGHTS AND ADVOCACY FOR CHILDREN WITH SPECIAL NEEDS

Legal rights serve as the cornerstone of a child's journey toward a life that embraces inclusion, equality, and opportunities for growth. Through advocacy for these rights, we ensure every child's potential is recognized, nurtured, and protected.

Individualized Education Plans (IEPs) - These are not just educational documents; they are legal mandates that delineate specific educational goals, accommodations, and services tailored to a child's unique needs. Understanding the IEP process and your child's rights within it is empowering. It allows you to actively engage in your child's education, ensuring their learning experience is optimized for success.

Americans with Disabilities Act (ADA) - This landmark legislation is a shield against discrimination based on disability. Understanding its provisions empowers you to advocate for your child's rights across various settings. Whether it is in the realm of education or ensuring access to public spaces, knowing the ADA is like having a legal compass to navigate the challenges your child may face.

Equality Act 2010 and Comparable Legislation – In the UK, you find the Equality Act 2010, and in many countries, you will find legislation with similar provisions, though the name might differ. These laws usually address the rights of individuals with disabilities or special needs. Familiarizing yourself with your country's specific legislation to secure your child's rights is imperative. These laws lay the foundation for inclusive and accessible environments that are vital for children with special needs.

EMPOWERING ADVOCACY: CREATING A BRIGHTER FUTURE

When nurturing children with special needs, advocacy is the thread that weaves together their rights, available resources, and opportunities. It is the active step in ensuring that the legal protections and provisions are not just words on paper but a living reality in your child's life.

Arming Ourselves with Knowledge - Advocacy starts with understanding the rights and legislation in place to protect your child. The knowledge gained empowers you to be an effective advocate, making you well-equipped to navigate systems, articulate your child's needs, and collaborate with relevant authorities.

Advocating for Our Child's Rights – It is more than just understanding; it is about taking action. As parents and caregivers, advocating for your child's rights means speaking up, engaging with educational institutions, and ensuring that your child receives the support they need. It means being a voice for your child when they may not have one.

Accessing Available Support - Advocacy opens doors to the support available for your child. By actively engaging in this process, you ensure your child can access the resources to help them thrive. Whether it is additional classroom support, accommodations, or therapy services, advocacy can be the bridge that connects your child with these vital resources.

By creating a foundation of advocacy, you are propelling your child towards a future filled with possibilities. You are not just securing their legal rights; you are paving the way for them to grow, learn, and thrive in a world that embraces and supports their unique journey. Advocacy is a powerful force that transforms the legal rights on paper into real opportunities for a brighter future.

REFLECTION

Have you thoroughly familiarized yourself with the legal rights and regulations related to your child's special needs, ensuring you can effectively advocate for him/her?

_____

_____

_____

_____

_____

How can you actively engage in the Individualized Education Plan (IEP) process to better advocate for your child's unique educational needs?

_____

_____

_____

_____

_____

Are you fully aware of the specific legislation in your country that addresses the rights and needs of individuals with disabilities?

_____

_____

_____

_____

_____

Are you taking advantage of the resources and support available under these laws?

_____

_____

_____

_____

_____

AFFIRMATIONS:

1. I am a knowledgeable and effective advocate for my child's rights and well-being, ensuring they receive the support they need to thrive.
2. I embrace the legal protections in place for my child with special needs, using them as a powerful tool to create a brighter future.
3. Through active advocacy, I transform legal rights into real opportunities, empowering my child to reach their full potential.

THOUGHTS TO PONDER

"Speak up for those who cannot speak for themselves, for the rights of all who are destitute." (Proverbs 31:8 - NIV).

"We must always take sides. Neutrality helps the oppressor, never the victim. Silence encourages the tormentor, never the tormented." —Elie Wiesel

NOTE TO SELF

_____

_____

_____

_____

_____

SELF-CARE CORNER - SELF-TALK

I've got this! Navigating the legal and financial aspects of supporting my child with special needs may seem overwhelming, but remember, I am armed with knowledge and determination. As I embark on this journey, by actively advocating for my child's rights, I am securing their legal protections and paving the way for a brighter future filled with possibilities. I will stay focused, stay informed, and be the voice that ensures that my child's unique path is recognized and supported every step of the way.

CHAPTER 10

TOOLS FOR EMPOWERMENT

In a world marked by rapid technological advancements, the tools available for empowering children with special needs are expanding at an unprecedented pace. Technology is not just a mere tool; it is a powerful conduit for inclusion, communication, and growth. In this chapter, we embark on a journey into the transformative realm of assistive technologies, innovative applications, and thriving online communities that are redefining the landscape of support and knowledge-sharing for families, caregivers, and children.

ASSISTIVE TECHNOLOGIES AND APPLICATIONS

Assistive technologies emerge as contemporary heroes in the lives of children with special needs, bridging the chasm between their abilities and the opportunities they deserve. These innovative solutions open doors to independence, communication, and active engagement, thereby unlocking a world of endless possibilities.

Communication Aids - One of the most remarkable achievements of assistive technology is the development of augmentative and alternative communication (AAC) devices. These remarkable tools provide a voice to nonverbal children, enabling them to express their thoughts, needs, and emotions.

These devices empower children to participate in conversations and activities with confidence. The transformative impact of AAC devices cannot be overstated. They allow children to bridge the gap between their inner and external worlds, offering them newfound independence and autonomy. This technological advancement fosters better communication and enhances self-esteem, ultimately contributing to improved quality of life for these children.

Educational Apps - The digital age brings forth a wealth of educational applications that cater to diverse learning styles and abilities. These interactive apps offer engaging ways to develop skills, enhance cognitive abilities, and encourage creativity. Educational apps have revolutionized the way children with special needs access and process information. Tailored to different learning styles and challenges, these apps transform the learning experience into an interactive, fun, and effective journey. They bridge educational gaps, making learning more accessible, engaging, and effective. Additionally, they empower children to progress at their own pace, building their confidence and self-reliance.

ONLINE COMMUNITIES AND PLATFORMS FOR SUPPORT AND KNOWLEDGE SHARING

In today's interconnected world, online communities serve as lifelines for parents, caregivers, and educators. They are spaces where individuals unite to share their experiences, seek advice, and offer support. These platforms are not merely virtual; they serve as extensions of real-world connections, providing comfort, insights, and a profound sense of belonging.

Support Networks - Online support groups can offer a safe haven where individuals can share their triumphs, challenges, and insights. Connecting with others who walk a similar path provides a powerful sense of camaraderie and reassurance. These digital support networks extend beyond geographical boundaries, linking people from diverse backgrounds who share a common goal – providing the best possible support and care for their loved ones with special needs. Here, individuals find solace in knowing they are not alone on their journey. They exchange experiences, provide emotional support, and offer valuable advice. These communities are a source of inspiration, demonstrating the resilience and strength of the human spirit in the face of adversity.

Knowledge Sharing - Online platforms represent treasure troves of information, resources, and expert insights. From research articles to practical tips, these digital hubs empower parents and caregivers with the knowledge and tools needed to make informed decisions. In an age where information is readily accessible, these platforms become invaluable resources. They provide access to the latest research, evidence-based practices, and tried-and-true strategies for nurturing children with special needs. The wealth of knowledge available online enables parents and caregivers to make well-informed choices and tailor their approaches to best suit the needs of their children.

EMPOWERING POSSIBILITIES AND SHAPING THE FUTURE

Technology and innovation are powerful catalysts for empowerment. They serve as gateways to a future where every child's potential is maximized, their voice is amplified, and their abilities are celebrated. By embracing assistive technologies, exploring educational applications, and actively engaging in online communities, we are collectively shaping a landscape of inclusion, support, and boundless opportunity.

In an ever-evolving digital landscape, the possibilities for empowerment continue to expand. The tools available are transforming the lives of children with special needs and redefining how their parents and caregivers provide support. The key to harnessing the full potential of these technological advancements lies in our willingness to adapt, learn, and collaborate. As we navigate this chapter of the special needs journey, we must remain open to the exciting possibilities that technology and innovation offer. We should recognize that these tools are not just instruments but enablers, paving the way for brighter, more inclusive futures.

Empowering possibilities through technology and innovation involves a combination of active participation and an open mindset. The landscape is constantly evolving, so it is vital to remain adaptable and curious. Be ready to explore new assistive technologies as they emerge, discover innovative applications that align with your child's needs, and seek out online communities where you can share your experiences and learn from others. The support and resources available today are more abundant than ever before. It is a promising era where the potential for growth and development is truly boundless.

The transformative impact of technology and innovation is evident in the lives of children with special needs. These advancements are not just tools but bridges to a world of opportunities. The possibilities for independence, communication, and growth are unfolding before us, and our collective responsibility is to embrace and nurture them. By incorporating assistive technologies, educational applications, and active participation in online communities into our journey, we are shaping a future where inclusion knows no bounds, where abilities are celebrated, and where the voices of children with special needs resonate louder than ever before.

REFLECTION

How can you embrace and adapt to the ever-evolving landscape of technology and innovation to better support your child with special needs?

_____

_____

_____

_____

_____

In what ways can assistive technologies and applications positively impact the life of your child or the children you care for?

_____

_____

_____

_____

What are the most valuable insights and experiences you have gained from engaging in online communities that support families and caregivers of children with special needs?

_____

_____

_____

_____

_____

How can you foster a culture of continuous learning and exploration to ensure you stay at the forefront of empowering possibilities for your child and family?

_____

_____

_____

_____

_____

AFFIRMATIONS

1. I embrace the boundless opportunities that technology and innovation offer to empower children with special needs, and I commit to adapting and learning as the landscape evolves.
2. Assistive technologies and applications open doors to independence, communication, and growth for my child, and I am grateful for their transformative impact on his/her life.
3. Engaging in online communities connects me with a network of support, knowledge, and inspiration, and I am proud to be part of this nurturing community.

THOUGHTS TO PONDER

"Have I not commanded you? Be strong and courageous. Do not be afraid, and do not be discouraged, for the Lord your God will be with you wherever you go." (Joshua 1:9 – NIV).

"For people without disabilities, technology makes things easier. For people with disabilities, technology makes things possible."
—*IBM Training Manual 1991*

NOTE TO SELF

_____

_____

_____

_____

_____

SELF-CARE CORNER

Here is an opportunity to create your own self-care expression by drawing.

CHAPTER 11

SELF-CARE FOR CAREGIVERS

When nurturing children with special needs, parents and caregivers often find themselves playing multiple roles—advocate, educator, therapist, and constant source of love and support. Amidst the responsibilities and demands of caregiving, it is crucial to remember that your well-being is the cornerstone upon which everything else rests. This chapter is an exploration of self-care—a sanctuary where caregivers can replenish, recharge, and find solace. By prioritizing your well-being, you fortify yourself to continue nurturing the lives of those you hold dear.

The Role of Caregivers in a Child's Journey - Caregivers are the unsung heroes in the lives of children with special needs. Their love, dedication, and steadfast support form the bedrock of a child's journey towards a fulfilling life. However, the journey of caregiving, though profoundly rewarding, is not without its challenges. It can be emotionally and physically taxing. Caregivers often find themselves stretching their limits, juggling multiple roles, and putting their own needs on the back burner. In the process of caring for their children, caregivers may sometimes neglect to care for themselves.

STRATEGIES FOR MANAGING CAREGIVER STRESS AND BURNOUT

Caregiving is a labor of love—a dedication that demands energy, resilience, and commitment. Yet, amidst the boundless love, it is essential to recognize the signs of stress and burnout and employ strategies to safeguard your own well-being.

Self-Reflection and Awareness - Take moments to check in with yourself. Recognize the signs of stress: emotional exhaustion, fatigue, and irritability, and prioritize self-care when needed. Self-awareness is the first step towards ensuring that you don't ignore your own well-being. Regularly assess your own mental and emotional state. When you notice signs of stress or burnout, don't sweep them under the rug. Acknowledge these feelings and consider them as signals that it is time to prioritize self-care.

Establishing Boundaries - Set clear boundaries between caregiving and personal time. Dedicate moments to yourself, whether it is a quiet walk, hobby, or cherished activity that brings you joy. Boundaries are crucial to prevent burnout. It is easy to lose yourself in caregiving, but establishing boundaries allows you to reclaim some time and space for yourself. This doesn't mean neglecting your responsibilities; rather, it means being intentional about setting aside time for self-care without guilt or hesitation.

BALANCING PERSONAL AND CAREGIVING RESPONSIBILITIES

The tightrope walk between personal responsibilities and caregiving duties requires finesse—a delicate balance that ensures your well-being remains intact. Balancing these facets of life enables you to offer your best self to both roles.

Time Management - Organize your time in a way that allocates dedicated moments for both caregiving and personal activities. Prioritize self-care as you would any other responsibility. Time management is a valuable skill for caregivers. Schedule your day to ensure you have time for your caregiving duties and your personal activities. This might mean seeking help or respite care to free up some of your time for self-care.

Seeking Support - Reach out for support from family, friends, or support groups. Building a network that understands and empathizes with your journey provides a safety net during challenging times. You don't have to go through this journey alone. Seek support from friends and family who understand your role as a caregiver. Consider joining support groups or seeking professional help when necessary.

NURTURING YOURSELF

When it comes to caregiving, your well-being is of paramount importance. By nurturing yourself—mind, body, and spirit—you cultivate the resilience, strength, and love that sustain you on this extraordinary journey.

It is important to remember that self-care is not a luxury but a necessity. When caregivers prioritize their well-being, they are better equipped to provide the care and support their children need.

Caregiving is a profound act of love and dedication. It can also be physically and emotionally demanding. Caregivers play many roles, from advocate to therapist, and often place the needs of their children above their own. However, neglecting self-care can lead to stress and burnout, ultimately affecting both the caregiver and the child.

Through self-reflection, boundary setting, and balancing personal and caregiving responsibilities, caregivers can mitigate the impact of stress and burnout. By seeking support and nurturing themselves, caregivers renew their strength and maintain the ability to provide love and support to their children.

Prioritizing Your Well-being - Self-care is not an act of selfishness; it is an act of self-preservation, and should be treated accordingly. Make yourself a priority, and do not feel guilty about it. You deserve to be prioritized by yourself and for yourself.

The Importance of Self-Care – The well-being of caregivers directly impacts the quality of care they can provide to their children. When caregivers prioritize their own physical, emotional, and mental health, they become better equipped to meet the needs of their children.

Renewal Through Self-Care - Nurturing yourself is an act of renewal. It is a way to recharge and replenish your inner resources, ensuring you can continue providing the care and support your child needs. As a caregiver, your well-being is a precious gift to both yourself and your child.

Self-care is an ongoing journey. It requires continuous effort and attention to your own needs. Prioritizing your well-being is not just an act of love for yourself but an act of love for your child.

It is a way to ensure that you can continue providing the support and care your child deserves.

FINDING YOUR SANCTUARY IN SELF-CARE

Self-care is not a luxury but a sanctuary where caregivers can find solace and strength. It is a place where you can recharge and renew, ensuring you remain a source of support and love for your child.

REFLECTION

How well do you currently balance your caregiving responsibilities and personal self-care time?

_____

_____

_____

_____

_____

What signs of stress and burnout have you observed in yourself, and how can you address them effectively?

_____

_____

_____

_____

What self-care activities bring you the most joy and relaxation, and how can you prioritize them in your daily life?

_____

_____

_____

_____

_____

_____

In what ways can you seek and accept support from your network of family and friends to lighten your caregiving load and promote your well-being?

_____

_____

_____

_____

_____

AFFIRMATIONS

1. I recognize that self-care is essential for both my well-being and the well-being of my child. It is not selfish but necessary.
2. I embrace self-care as a sanctuary for renewal and strength, ensuring I can continue providing support and love to my child.
3. I prioritize self-awareness, setting boundaries, and seeking support as valuable strategies for managing caregiver stress and maintaining my health.

THOUGHTS TO PONDER

"Love your neighbor as yourself." (Mark 12:31 - NIV).

"Self-care is never a selfish act—it is simply good stewardship of the only gift I have, the gift I was put on earth to offer to others." —Parker Palmer

NOTE SELF

_____

_____

_____

_____

_____

SELF-CARE CORNER - A JINGLE

In a world of innovation, we find our way,
Empowering children, come what may.
With technology's embrace, we stand tall,
Unlocking their potential, breaking down every wall.

Together we'll soar, reach new heights,
In this digital world, where the future ignites.
Assistive tools and knowledge at hand,
Shaping a landscape, where every child can stand.

From AAC devices, they find their voice,
Expressing thoughts, making their choice.
Educational apps, a journey so grand,
Learning with joy, hand in hand.

Together we'll soar, reach new heights,
In this digital world, where the future ignites.
Assistive tools and knowledge at hand,
Shaping a landscape, where every child can stand.

Online communities, a source of grace,

In this vast network, we find our place.
Support and knowledge, they're always near,
Uniting in love, banishing every fear.

Together we'll soar, reach new heights,
In this digital world, where the future ignites.
Assistive tools and knowledge at hand,
Shaping a landscape, where every child can stand.

So, let's embrace technology's boundless scope,
With open hearts and endless hope.
Empowering possibilities, we understand,
In this world of inclusion, hand in hand.

CHAPTER 12

EMPOWERING EFFECTIVE STRATEGIES

In the intricate mosaic of education, the ability to learn is a treasure—a key that unlocks doors to understanding, growth, and empowerment. For children with special needs, cultivating effective learning strategies is a journey of empowerment, providing them with tools to navigate information, process concepts, and engage with the world around them. This chapter is dedicated to exploring a range of strategies and techniques that foster effective learning, enabling children to confidently unravel the mysteries of knowledge and discovery.

NURTURING EFFECTIVE LEARNING STRATEGIES

Learning is a multifaceted journey, and each child's path is unique. Equipping children with strategies that resonate with their learning styles and abilities empowers them to navigate their educational voyage with confidence and enthusiasm.

Mnemonic Devices - Mnemonic devices are like secret codes that unlock the doors to memory. These clever tools use associations to help children remember information that might otherwise slip away. By teaching children to create vivid and imaginative associations, we empower them to retain information more effectively. For instance, when learning the order of mathematical operations, a phrase like "Please Excuse

My Dear Aunt Sally" (which stands for Parentheses, Exponents, Multiplication, Division, Addition, Subtraction) can be a fun and memorable mnemonic device.

These memory aids provide children with an imaginative and interactive way to remember information. Whether it is using acronyms, rhymes, or visual associations, mnemonics can be tailored to a child's interests and preferences. This makes learning more engaging and enhances memory retention, ensuring that important concepts and facts are never forgotten.

Framing Techniques - Framing is all about identifying and organizing critical content regarding a topic. Students would focus on the topic, reveal the main ideas, analyze the details, make a statement such as what is the relevance of this information, and extend understanding. Teaching students how to identify important information and why it is so helps them to filter important information to focus on. When tackling a history lesson, for example, they can learn to identify the main events and create a timeline to better understand the sequence of events.

The beauty of framing techniques lies in their adaptability to different subjects and learning styles. Children can create mind maps, outlines, or diagrams to organize information visually, helping them better understand complex topics. Moreover, these techniques foster critical thinking as they require children to analyze information and identify its core components.

PRODUCTIVITY HACKS FOR EFFECTIVE LEARNING

In a world filled with distractions and competing demands, productivity hacks become valuable allies in the quest for efficient learning. Teaching children strategies to manage their time, prioritize tasks, and optimize their learning environment equips them with the tools to harness their potential.

Task Prioritization - The ability to prioritize tasks is a vital skill. Teaching children to discern which tasks are most important and urgent empowers them to tackle challenges systematically and stay on course with their learning goals. For example, when working on homework, they can identify which assignments need immediate attention and which can be completed later, avoiding the stress of last-minute rushes.

Task prioritization goes beyond academic settings; it is a skill that serves children well throughout their lives. Whether it is organizing their daily routines, managing work responsibilities, or handling personal tasks, this skill ensures they make the most of their time and resources.

Reward-Based Learning - The psychology of rewards is a powerful motivator. By helping children understand that they can complete essential tasks before indulging in preferred activities, such as playing video games or going out with friends, we encourage a sense of accomplishment and motivation. This strategy can work wonders in promoting focus and productivity.

Reward-based learning is not just about incentives but also about building a sense of responsibility and discipline. It teaches children that they can achieve their goals and enjoy the fruits of their labor with effort and focus. This sense of achievement is a powerful motivator that extends beyond learning and into all aspects of life.

EMPOWERMENT THROUGH LEARNING

As we journey through the realm of effective learning strategies, we empower children with a toolkit that transcends textbooks and classrooms. By nurturing mnemonic devices, framing techniques, and productivity hacks, we lay the foundation for a future where children are not just passive learners but active explorers and critical thinkers.

These strategies enable children to become more confident and independent learners. They empower them to approach challenges with a problem-solving mindset, seek solutions, and explore their interests and passions. This approach doesn't just equip them for academic success but also for life beyond the classroom.

These learning strategies are not exhaustive; there are many more. Nevertheless, they open doors to a world of possibilities for children with special needs. They enable them to uncover their unique talents, to understand and overcome challenges, and to become lifelong learners who approach the world with curiosity and confidence. By nurturing these strategies, we lay the foundation for their journey of empowerment, where the pursuit of knowledge is not just a path but a lifelong adventure.

REFLECTION

How can you tailor mnemonic devices to suit your child's interests and enhance his/her learning experience?

_____

_____

_____

_____

_____

What framing techniques can you introduce to help your child better understand complex subjects and concepts?

_____

_____

_____

_____

How can you teach your child effective task prioritization, not only for academics but also for life skills?

_____

_____

_____

_____

_____

In what ways can you incorporate reward-based learning to motivate your child to stay focused and achieve his/her goals?

_____

_____

_____

_____

_____

AFFIRMATIONS

1. I am committed to nurturing effective learning strategies that empower my child to embrace knowledge and discovery.
2. I believe in my child's ability to become a confident and independent learner through tailored mnemonic devices and framing techniques.
3. I encourage my child to approach challenges with a problem-solving mindset and an open heart, knowing that learning is an exciting lifelong adventure.

THOUGHTS TO PONDER

"Do your best to present yourself to God as one approved, a worker who does not need to be ashamed and who correctly handles the word of truth." (2 Timothy 2:15 – NIV).

"Tell me and I forget, teach me and I may remember, involve me and I learn." —Benjamin Franklin

NOTE TO SELF

_____

_____

_____

_____

_____

SELF-CARE CORNER - A DIALOGUE BETWEEN A FATHER AND DAUGHTER

Dad: Hey there, sweetheart! How was school today? Anything interesting?

Emma: Hi, Dad! School was good, and I learned about some cool new learning strategies.

Dad: Learning strategies? That sounds intriguing! Tell me more. What did you learn today?

Emma: Well, we talked about mnemonic devices. They're like secret codes to remember stuff. We even learned one for remembering math operations. It's "Please Excuse My Dear Aunt Sally." See, it stands for Parentheses, Exponents, Multiplication, Division, Addition, Subtraction.

Dad: Wow, that's clever! I'll have to remember that one myself. _(Smiles)_ What else did you discuss?

Emma: We also talked about framing techniques. It's all about identifying the main points. Like when I'm doing a history assignment, I can make a timeline to understand it better.

Dad: That's fantastic, honey. These techniques sound like they can make learning more engaging and effective. But tell me, are there any productivity hacks you learned?

Emma: Yes, Dad! We discussed task prioritization, which means figuring out what needs to be done first. It's not just for schoolwork but for everyday life too. And there's something called reward-based learning. It's like a fun way to motivate myself to finish tasks before enjoying my hobbies, like playing video games.

Dad: That's incredible, kiddo! Learning all these strategies will help you not only in school but also in life. Being able to organize your tasks, remember important things, and staying motivated are valuable skills.

Emma: Thanks, Dad! I'm excited to try them out and become a better learner.

Dad: I know you will, sweetheart. I'm here to help you along the way. Learning is a lifelong adventure, and I'm so proud of the curious and confident explorer you're becoming.

Emma: I love you, Dad.

Dad: I love you too, my smart and amazing girl.

CHAPTER 13

NURTURING FAITH AND RESILIENCE

AN EXPRESSION OF BELIEF

In the journey of parenting children with special needs, it is essential to find your source of strength and hope, regardless of your religious or spiritual beliefs. For me, that source has always been my faith in God. However, it is important to emphasize that this book is not exclusively for Christians. The principles and insights shared here can resonate with parents and caregivers of all backgrounds and beliefs. My intention in this chapter is to share how faith has played a pivotal role in my parenting journey and how it can serve as a powerful anchor of hope and resilience for anyone facing the unique challenges of nurturing children with special needs.

My faith in God has been the cornerstone upon which I have built my approach to parenting. It has enabled me to shift my mindset from one of fear and uncertainty to a proactive perspective filled with hope and optimism. This shift began when I realized that I was not alone in this journey. I found comfort in knowing that there was a higher power, a loving presence, that cared about my child's well-being just as much as I did.

A SOURCE OF STRENGTH AND HOPE

Parenting a child with special needs can be overwhelming at times. The daily challenges, the uncertainties about the future, and the constant advocacy required can take a toll on your emotional and mental well-being. It is during these moments of doubt and exhaustion that my faith has served as a wellspring of strength and hope.

Through prayer and reflection, I have drawn upon my faith to find the inner fortitude to keep moving forward. It is as if there is an unwavering assurance that everything will work out as it should, even when the path ahead seems shrouded in darkness. This sense of divine assurance has been my guiding light during some of the toughest times.

My faith has taught me that every child is a unique and precious gift. While it may be easy to focus on the limitations and challenges that come with special needs, faith reminds me of the limitless potential within every child. It encourages me to look beyond the diagnosis and see the untapped strengths, talents, and possibilities that lie within my child.

Dreaming with God for my child - One of the most beautiful aspects of faith is the belief in the power of dreams. As a parent, I have learned to dream with God for my child. I envision a future filled with growth, progress, and accomplishments tailored to my child's unique abilities and aspirations.

This shared dream with a higher power has given me a sense of purpose and direction. It has allowed me to set goals for my child that go beyond societal expectations or limitations imposed by a diagnosis. Instead, I strive to create an environment where my child can thrive, express themselves, and reach their full potential.

Accepting what is and working for a better tomorrow - Faith has also been instrumental in helping me accept the present reality while still working tirelessly for a better tomorrow. It is a delicate balance between embracing my child's current abilities and challenges and relentlessly pursuing opportunities for growth and development.

My faith reminds me that acceptance doesn't mean resignation; it means acknowledging the truth of the situation and finding ways to make the best of it. I have learned to celebrate every small victory, no matter how insignificant it may seem to others, knowing that each step forward is a testament to my child's resilience and my faith.

Strength and determination to partner with God - Raising a child with special needs is not a solitary endeavor. It is a partnership between a parent, a caregiver, and a higher power. My faith has given me the strength and determination to partner with God in this sacred journey of parenting.

I have come to understand that I am not alone in this task. God is with me every step of the way, providing guidance, wisdom, and the grace to face each day with hope and resilience. This partnership empowers me to tap into my child's strengths and help them grow into the unique individuals they are meant to be.

GOD'S ENABLING GRACE FOR THE JOURNEY

In our lives, we often encounter moments that secm insurmountable. Yet, during these very moments, we can tap into

God's enabling grace—a divine source of strength and abilities that empower us to navigate the challenges of raising a child with special needs. Enabling grace is a concept deeply rooted in faith, reminding us that we are never alone on this journey. It signifies the profound partnership between our human efforts and the divine support that God provides. This grace empowers us to take each step with determination and hope.

In the realm of parenting children with special needs, enabling grace manifests in various ways. It grants us the wisdom to make informed decisions, the patience to weather difficult days, and the resilience to keep moving forward. It is the assurance that we are equipped with the capabilities needed to provide the best care and support to our children. This enabling grace also extends to our children. It is a source of inner strength that helps them navigate their unique path. It empowers them to face their challenges with courage and resilience, allowing their individuality to shine brightly.

As parents and caregivers, we can nurture this enabling grace by staying connected with our faith and seeking moments of spiritual reflection. Prayer and meditation become essential tools in accessing the wellspring of strength that God provides. They enable us to draw upon divine wisdom and guidance as we make choices that impact our children's lives.

Moreover, enabling grace teaches us that we can do all things through our faith in God, who strengthens us. It encourages us to dream with boundless optimism, accept the present, and strive for a better tomorrow. It reminds us that our journey is not one of solitary endeavors but a partnership between our human efforts and divine support.

REFLECTION

How does your belief system provide you with strength and hope in your journey as a parent or caregiver of a child with special needs?

_____

_____

_____

_____

_____

Can you recall a specific moment when your faith or belief system helped you navigate a challenging situation with your child? What did you learn from that experience?

_____

_____

_____

_____

_____

In what ways can you integrate the concept of accepting the present while striving for a better tomorrow into your daily life as a parent or caregiver?

_____

_____

_____

_____

_____

AFFIRMATIONS

1. I draw strength and hope from my belief system, knowing that I am not alone on this journey of nurturing my child's potential.
2. My faith empowers me to dream with boundless optimism and see the limitless potential within my child.
3. I embrace the present, accepting it as the starting point for a better future, fueled by faith and determination.

THOUGHTS TO PONDER

"I can do all things through Christ who strengthens me." (Philippians 4:13 – NIV).

"Faith is taking the first step even when you don't see the whole staircase." —Martin Luther King Jr.

NOTE TO SELF

_____

_____

_____

_____

_____

SELF-CARE CORNER - PRAYER

Abba Father, in the journey of parenting children with special needs, we come before You with hearts full of gratitude. We thank You for the strength and hope that faith in Your love has provided.

As we face the challenges and uncertainties, we pray for the assurance that everything will work out as it should. Help us to dream with boundless optimism for our children, to accept the present, and to strive for a better tomorrow, knowing that we are partners in this sacred journey, guided by Your enabling grace. In Your name, we find the determination and resilience to face each day with hope. Amen.

CHAPTER 14

NOURISHMENT AND MEDICATION FOR YOUR CHILD'S HEALTH

As parents and caregivers of children with special needs, we often find ourselves navigating complex terrains when it comes to nutrition and medication. Our roles extend beyond the typical responsibilities of parenting as we become advocates, therapists, and the primary source of love and support for our children. In this chapter, we will explore the crucial aspects of nourishment and medication, recognizing that these areas pose unique challenges for our children, each with their own distinct personalities, preferences, strengths, and limitations.

NURTURING EFFECTIVE NUTRITION

Nutrition is the cornerstone of a child's physical and cognitive development. It fuels their growth, supports their immune system, and helps them thrive. However, children with special needs may present us with specific nutritional challenges, often tied to their unique diagnoses and individual tastes.

It is important to remember that our children are more than their diagnoses; they have their own distinct preferences when it comes to food. Some may be fixated on specific items and resist trying new foods, while others might be more adventurous eaters. As caregivers, we are often in a delicate dance of balancing nutritional needs with individual tastes.

PATIENCE AND UNDERSTANDING

The key to addressing these variations in appetite and dietary preferences is to approach mealtime with patience and understanding. It can be frustrating when our children insist on eating the same meal daily or refuse to try new foods. However, it is crucial not to direct our frustration toward them. Instead, we should consider the following principles:

- *Simplicity and Variety* - Striking a balance is key. While it is essential to keep meals simple, it is equally important to offer a variety of options that incorporate foods meeting nutritional requirements while respecting their tastes.

- *Creativity* - Sometimes, creativity is necessary to ensure our children receive the necessary nutrients. We might need to blend vegetables into a smoothie, hide them in sauces, or make appealing shapes with food. The goal is to make nutritious meals more attractive to our children.

- *Supplements* - In certain cases, supplements may be required to bridge nutritional gaps. It is crucial to consult with healthcare professionals to determine if supplements are necessary and, if so, to identify suitable ones.

Our children's growth and development depend significantly on proper nutrition. As caregivers, we need to be patient and persistent in our efforts to provide a balanced diet that supports their dietary needs while accommodating their preferences. Every child is unique, and their dietary journey will reflect that uniqueness.

TAILORED APPROACHES TO MEDICATION

When it comes to medication for children with special needs, there is no one-size-fits-all solution. Each child may respond differently to various treatments, and it is essential to understand that if medication is required, it is generally better to medicate than not.

Parents often hesitate when it comes to medication, primarily if they have had prior experiences where they believed a medication caused adverse effects. However, it is essential to recognize the complexity of the relationship between medication and its effects. Yes, medications do cause adverse effects, so care must be taken, and if an alternative is present, then that should be utilized. Also, when one child has an adverse effect from a specific medication, it does not mean your child will too.

Quality of life plays a significant role in decisions about medication. Many conditions requiring medication can significantly improve with proper treatment, leading to better overall well-being for our children.

CONSIDERATIONS FOR MEDICATION

Due Diligence - Parents should conduct thorough research and consult with healthcare professionals to understand the benefits, risks, and potential side effects of any medication prescribed for their child. Knowledge is empowering and helps in making informed decisions.

Open-Mindedness - Approach treatment with an open mind. While medication may be necessary, explore alternative therapies such as behavior therapy, counseling, or natural remedies if they align with your child's specific needs. The goal is to improve your child's overall well-being.

Individualized Care - Each child is unique, and their response to medication will be unique as well. What works for one child may not work for another. Be patient in finding the right treatment plan tailored to your child's needs.

Monitoring - Regularly monitor your child's progress while on medication. Maintain open communication with healthcare providers, sharing any concerns or observations you may have.

Overall, as parents and caregivers of children with special needs, we face unique challenges in the realms of nutrition and medication. It is essential to approach these aspects of care with compassion, patience, and an open mind. Our children's health and well-being should always be the primary focus, and our dedication to meeting their unique needs will undoubtedly make a significant difference in their life journey. Remember that you are not alone; seek support and guidance from healthcare professionals and support networks to ensure the best possible care for your child.

REFLECTIONS

How can you best balance the nutritional needs of your child with special preferences and dietary challenges?

_____

_____

_____

_____

_____

What steps can you take to approach mealtimes with more patience and understanding when your child resists trying new foods?

_____

_____

_____

_____

_____

How can you stay open-minded and well-informed when considering medication for your child with special needs?

_____

_____

_____

_____

_____

What alternative therapies and treatments might complement or replace medication for your child, and how can you explore these options further?

_____

_____

_____

_____

_____

AFFIRMATIONS

1. I am patient and persistent in providing a balanced diet that supports my child's dietary needs and individual preferences.
2. I approach medication decisions with an open mind, seeking the best possible solutions to improve my child's overall well-being.
3. I am an advocate for my child's unique needs and will tirelessly seek the best solutions to nurture their health and happiness.

THOUGHTS TO PONDER

"But he was pierced for our transgressions, he was crushed for our iniquities; the punishment that brought us peace was on him, and by his wounds, we are healed." (Isaiah 53:5 – NIV).

"Healing is a matter of time, but it is sometimes also a matter of opportunity." —Hippocrates

NOTE TO SELF

_____

_____

_____

_____

_____

SELF-CARE CORNER - A MENTAL PICTURE

Imagine you are a caring gardener tending to a unique garden, each plant representing a child with special needs. Your watering can is filled with patience, and your nurturing touch is understanding. Just like each plant has its own characteristics and needs, so do our children.

Nutrition is the sunlight that helps them grow. Some may thrive on familiar soil, while others need a mix of different elements. It is about finding the right balance between simplicity and variety. Get creative—maybe you will have to blend some veggies into a "nutrient smoothie" or shape food into fun forms. When it is necessary, supplements are like plant vitamins to fill in the gaps.

Medication is the gentle rain that can help them bloom. Remember, what works for one plant might not work for another. Be diligent in your research, consult with experts, and be open-minded. Sometimes, the right treatment can make all the difference in their well-being.

Just as a beautiful garden requires time, attention, and unique care for each plant, our children need our dedication, love, and willingness to adapt to their individuality. You are not alone on this gardening journey. Seek help when needed, and your garden of children will flourish and thrive.

CONCLUSION

EMBRACING THE JOURNEY OF LOVE, GROWTH, AND POSSIBILITY

There exists a journey marked by love, resilience, and an unwavering belief in the potential of every child. As we draw the final threads of this book together, we find ourselves with insights, strategies, and encouragement that illuminate the path of nurturing children with special needs. This journey, intricately woven with chapters that touch upon diverse aspects, reflects the multi-dimensional nature of caregiving, advocacy, and empowerment.

At the heart of this journey lies the profound art of embracing a courageous act that transcends grief and transforms it into acceptance. We have explored the delicate balance of navigating the spectrum of emotions that follow a diagnosis, a journey that shifts from mourning a vision of what could have been to celebrating the unique possibilities of every child. Through the chapters of grieving, mindset cultivation, skillset development, and celebration of progress, we have witnessed the emergence of a resilient spirit that nurtures, supports, and empowers.

The chapters on mindset and skillset have echoed the sentiment that empowerment is a dance—a harmonious interplay of belief in possibility and the practical tools that pave the way for growth.

From fostering positive attitudes to cultivating resilience, from nurturing physical well-being to empowering communication, we have embraced the delicate balance of nurturing a holistic foundation upon which children with special needs can thrive.

Inclusive education and advocacy, forming the cornerstone of our journey, have illuminated the path toward a world where every child's potential is recognized and celebrated. From advocating for inclusive education rights to forging collaborations between parents, teachers, and specialists, we have created a chorale of voices that champion the importance of inclusivity—a world where diversity is not only acknowledged but celebrated.

Technology and innovation, coupled with the power of faith, have served as vibrant threads that enrich the narrative. Through assistive technologies and online communities, we have harnessed the tools of modernity to create spaces of empowerment and support. In honoring the place of faith, we have celebrated the diverse paths that individuals embark upon, each anchored by hope, resilience, and a belief in a future of boundless possibilities.

As we conclude, we forge a legacy of empowerment, inclusion, and unyielding belief. Just as a tapestry is composed of countless threads, each unique yet harmoniously intertwined, so is the journey of nurturing children with special needs—a testament to the collective efforts of parents, caregivers, and advocates who have persevered with love, achieved growth, and experienced grand possibilities.

I pray that this book serves as a guide, a lantern that lights the path for those who walk alongside children with special needs, and that you will refer back to relevant sections as the need arises. As you navigate this journey, remember that you are not alone. You are part of a community made up of individuals united by a common purpose—to empower, uplift, and celebrate the extraordinary lives of these remarkable children. You may join my online community at www.hannahmoments.com.

As you embrace the journey, may you find strength in moments of challenge, joy in every victory, and a profound sense of fulfillment in nurturing a future where every child can flourish. The threads of your dedication, love, and unwavering belief will forever shine as a beacon of hope and possibility. May the Lord be with you always as you continue your journey of embracing possibilities, nurturing children with special needs.

ABOUT THE AUTHOR

Meet Vanesia Bowden, a remarkable woman who wears many hats. As a special needs mom, her personal journey has shaped her into a compassionate advocate and caregiver for children with unique requirements. She understands the challenges, hopes, and dreams of fellow parents navigating the world of special needs.

Vanesia Bowden is more than just a dedicated mother. She is a seasoned pharmacist with a wealth of knowledge about health, medication, and the intricacies of managing medicine. Her unparalleled expertise in this field makes her an invaluable resource for families seeking guidance.

In addition to her role as a pharmacist, Vanesia Bowden is an accomplished educator and trainer. Her passion for teaching extends to empowering others with the knowledge they need to create a better world for children with special needs. As a certified cognitive coach, she has honed the skills necessary to guide parents and caregivers through the often-complex realm of neurodiversity.

Vanesia Bowden is also an author and speaker. Her words carry the weight of experience and expertise, offering insights and inspiration to others on similar journeys. Her messages are powerful and resonate with anyone seeking guidance on nurturing and supporting children with unique requirements.

Vanesia Bowden's unique position at the intersection of health and education is where her heart lies. She is a champion for the cause of special needs children, working tirelessly to bridge gaps and provide the support and resources necessary for their growth and well-being.

In a world where special needs parenting can be challenging and complex, Vanesia is a beacon of hope, knowledge, and strength. Her qualifications, certifications, and experience make her a formidable force for positive change in the lives of the families she touches. With Vanesia by your side, you have a dedicated advocate, educator, and coach committed to helping you embrace the possibilities that special needs parenting offers.

REFERENCES

1. Aunola, K., Nurmi, J. E., Onatsu-Arvilommi, T., & Pulkkinen, L. (1999). The role of parents' self-esteem, mastery-orientation and social background in their parenting styles. *Scandinavian journal of psychology, 40*(4), 307–317. https://doi.org/10.1111/1467-9450.404131

2. Batiz, C. M. (2022). *An examination of the influence of parental mindset, involvement, and experience on student mindset and musical experience* (Order No. 29326834). Available from ProQuest One Academic. (2702516668). Retrieved from https://www.proquest.com/dissertations-theses/examination-influence-parental-mindset/docview/2702516668/se-2

3. DiLonardo, M. J. (2023). *Deep Breathing: Relax and Ease Stress.* WebMD. https://www.webmd.com/parenting/how-to-deep-breathe

4. *Eatwell Guide: How to eat a healthy balanced diet.* (n.d.). Www.nhsinform.scot. https://www.nhsinform.scot/healthy-living/food-and-nutrition/eating-well/eatwell-guide-how-to-eat-a-healthy-balanced-diet/

5. Fusar-Poli, P., Salazar de Pablo, G., De Micheli, A., Nieman, D. H., Correll, C. U., Kessing, L. V., Pfennig, A., Bechdolf, A., Borgwardt, S., Arango, C., & Van Amelsvoort, T. (2020). What is good mental health? A scoping review. *European Neuropsychopharmacology, 31,* 33–46. https://doi.org/10.1016/j.euroneuro.2019.12.105

6. Schramayr, E. (2018, Dec 05). The importance of mindset. *The Spectator* Retrieved from https://www.proquest.com/newspapers/importance-mindset/docview/2149627111/se-2